AFRICAN ORIGINS OF MONOTHEISM

AFRICAN ORIGINS
of MONOTHEISM

Challenging the Eurocentric Interpretation
of God Concepts on the Continent and in Diaspora

GWINYAI H. MUZOREWA

◆PICKWICK *Publications* • Eugene, Oregon

AFRICAN ORIGINS OF MONOTHEISM
Challenging the Eurocentric Interpretation of God Concepts on the Continent and in Diaspora

Copyright © 2014 Gwinyai H. Muzorewa. All rights reserved. Except for brief quotations in critical publications or reviews, no part of this book may be reproduced in any manner without prior written permission from the publisher. Write: Permissions, Wipf and Stock Publishers, 199 W. 8th Ave., Suite 3, Eugene, OR 97401.

Pickwick Publications
An imprint of Wipf and Stock Publishers
199 W. 8th Ave., Suite 3
Eugene, OR 97401

www.wipfandstock.com

ISBN 13: 978-1-623032-310-6

Cataloging-in-Publication data:

Muzorewa, Gwinyai H.

African origins of monotheism : challenging the Eurocentric interpretation of God concepts on the continent and in diaspora / Gwinyai H. Muzorewa, with a foreword by Ralph C. Watkins.

x + 106 p. ; 23 cm. Includes bibliographical references and index.

ISBN 13: 978-1-62032-310-6

1. God. 2. Theology, Doctrinal—Africa, Sub-Saharan. 3. Africa—Religion. I. Watkins, Ralph C. II. Title.

BT103 M89 2014

Manufactured in the U.S.A.

This book is dedicated to all our grandchildren: Caleb, Noah (Fungai and Tony Bennett's), and Asher (Rudo and Charles Hughes'), and the yet-unborn, because I want our grandchildren to know that Africa is the cradle of human civilization and originality, universality, and godliness. To this one God my wife and I have always had unwavering allegiance to monotheism, which symbolizes unity of divinity, love, omniscience, and power.

CONTENTS

Foreword by Ralph C. Watkins · ix
1 Introduction · 1
2 African Origins of Monotheism · 9
3 African Theological Concepts of God · 35
4 God Concept in African Diaspora · 50
5 God, Good, and Evil · 67
6 Theologizing a God Concept · 81
Bibliography · 91
Name Index · 99
Topical Index · 101
Scripture Index · 105

FOREWORD

THE TEXT PUSHES THE boundaries of the historical sources and social constructs of religious history and concepts of God. Dr. Gwinyai Muzorewa opens up the historical sources to transcend the limits of Eurocentric hegemony over the monotheistic concept of God. By aggressively and persuasively arguing that the origins of monotheism are African in root and fruit, the conversation about God is reframed. The reader is made to step outside the normal Eurocentric constructs of Western views of God and see an African concept as its predecessor and footnote. The constructs of monotheism are distinguished in the work as "cognitive monotheism" as opposed to "contractual monotheism." Muzorewa's argument rests on the construct of cognitive monotheism that he argues is the root of the construct that is founded in Africa. Rightly placing this monotheistic construct throughout the continent and not just in Egypt is central to the book's argument, and rightly so, as the claim in the book is that this construct of monotheism flourished across the continent of Africa.

The second step in Muzorewa's argument is the ways in which monotheism is expressed across time and space on the continent of Africa. He successfully builds his argument and gives the reader a view of God in Egypt, Zambia, Tanzania, Mozambique, Kenya, Malawi, Rwanda, Burundi, Congo, Angola, Cote D'Ivoire, Ghana, Zimbabwe, Lesotho, South Africa, Botswana, Uganda, Nigeria, Ethiopia and the Sudan. While the work is inclusive of a wide array of countries in Africa, it does not diminish them or descend into making them identical. The text deals delicately with the nuances and names for God while helping the reader see the commonalities of how monotheism emerges in each unique African cultural context. The writer gives the reader a detailed tour of the theological landscape of Africa while not shying from the areas of theological conversation that don't fit in nice, neat categories in terms of Western constructs. He is not afraid to deal with hard questions and points of tension in the concept of God across the continent. A major strength of the book is that it challenges Western constructs as it provides the reader with new language to have a conversation about African concepts of God.

The African Diaspora is defined and used as the table upon which the theological conversation takes place in the book. The ancestors are brought into the conversation with respect, intellectual integrity, and a reframing of how ancestors and death, which is life, are seen in an African context. The misunderstanding in the Western world about the role of the ancestors is corrected in this book. The beauty in the writing is that Dr. Muzorewa does not come off as defensive in his work. The work is instructive and the argument builds as he challenges perceptions previously held by Eurocentric scholars and provides an African frame by which to see the ancestors in a positive and appropriate light. Finally, the book gives us a more complete sense of how African and Africans in the Diaspora understand and define who God is for them. This book will fill a void in our field and is worthy of immediate publication. I would assign it to my students.

Ralph C. Watkins, DMin, PhD
Associate Professor of Society, Religion, and Africana Studies
Assistant Dean, The Center for the Study of Africana Religion and Culture
Fuller Theological Seminary

one

INTRODUCTION

GOD'S SELF-REVELATION IS AMONG the most reliable channels by which humanity may know and even begin to comprehend the nature of the living God. This is true of humanity as well as any other creatures to which God chooses to reveal divinity. Human awareness and sense of not only the existence but ontological reality of the Ultimate also occurs through faith, experience, and/or cognitive knowledge, all made possible through God's self-revelation. Furthermore, discussions on the subject of God are endless because God continues to reveal who God is in various ways and circumstances to diverse communities. Subsequently, these communities name God and develop anthropomorphic as well as other attributes relative to the Reality they experienced. From these one can garner concepts of God.

Generally speaking, divine attributes are based on what God reveals to humanity and how such theophanies are conceived by the recipients. In Sub-Saharan Africa, for instance, the majority of the indigenous names of God are indicative of what God has revealed to a particular community. Understood from a traditional perspective expressed systematically and conceived via the medium of an African spirituality, the Great Spirit is best described as the Unknowable, self-revealing one. In this book the author will try to avoid assigning gender to God because the African concept of God presented here is neither male nor female. I would rather be faithful to this concern than any grammatical rules. Differently put, awkward grammar is to be preferred to misrepresenting God just because the English language has its limitations. Furthermore, in my language as well as other African languages, there is no place for either a "he" or "she" or "it" in reference to God. If I say in Shona, *Mwari ari kudenga*, literally God is in heaven, the word *ari* is more than neuter gender. It does not make reference to either male or female. Yet, it refers to a person, not a thing. I am comfortable with the notion that God is a person who is "Wholly Other." A casual glance at, not to mention careful scrutiny of, the attributes of God suggests that God is a Person, but nothing like you and me. God's perfection cannot be limited to either gender, or to both genders combined or tripled. In my opinion, scholars who maintain that God is both male and female still limit God to these characteristics. To say "Ultimate" supersedes all and any human categories the finite mind may conceive, unless it is revealed by God's own self.

Among monotheistic religions, Christianity claims to know God on the basis of five primary factors: (1) what God reveals to humanity in history (revelation); (2) what the word of God, that is, the Hebrew people's recorded witness of who God is, and what God says and does (Scripture); (3) what the church's creeds and traditions convey about who God is as the church professes its faith (tradition); (4) present personal or community experience of what God has done to manifest God's own glory, which has helped people to believe that the Lord is God (experience); (5) reason, whether aided with God's grace, revelation, or scientific observation (reason). But for Christianity in Africa two major sources of African theology should be added to this list, namely, (6) an African epistemology/culture that emanates from primitive divine revelation, and (7) traditional religiosity with all the "oral" sacred texts of theology, like prayer, proverbs, and myths (the primitive revelation of the Great Spirit God). It is for this reason that theology in Africa cannot be just like any other. There is need for this African component just as Scripture is a prerequisite for Christian theology wherever it is done.

With the exception of extreme biblicists like the late Dr. Byang Kato, many serious scholars agree that these two make an important addition to the people's knowledge of God. Dr. Kato "stressed the distinctiveness of the experience of the Christian Gospel to such an extent that he rejected the positive evaluation of any pre-Christian religious tradition as a distraction from the necessary 'emphasis on Bible truth.'"[1] Dr. Kato lost ground not only to more moderate scholars, but even to other evangelicals who had initially shared his view.

---

1. Bediako, "Understanding African Theology."

One of the conservative theologians on the continent writes, "It is now being recognized that African traditional religiosity is playing a major role in African understanding of Christian faith, in the rapid expansion of Christianity, and in the nature of pastoral problems faced by churches especially in the rural areas."[2] Many scholars note with interest that "African Christians are discovering, often with passionate interest, that there are many religious and cultural 'points of contact' between biblical and African backgrounds."[3] These "points of contact" compel this theologian to glean traditional theology, which enriches Christian theology and most certainly Christian worship. Based on the universality and specificity of the revelation, many Christians are freely utilizing God concepts from traditional religion because both faiths believe in the same God.

Scholars who use "Christ" as the reason to separate Christianity from any knowledge of God through traditional religion do well to bear in mind that Christ is the mediator not castigator. The word of God says, "For God did not send his son to condemn the world but to save the world through him" (John 3:17). Dr. Kwame Bediako alludes to this crucial observation when he discusses a desirable continuity between traditional religion and Christianity. He observed that "the African Church needed to build its bridges to the 'revelation' given to Africans in their pre-Christian and pre-missionary religious traditions of the past." Additionally, Bediako said that the intention was to "connect the 'old' and the 'new' in African religious experience."[4] Other scholars also agree with Bediako (Idowu, Setiloane, Kibicho, and Gaba).

The significance of this commonality far exceeds the danger of elements of syncretism. Syncretism is to be regarded as negative when a religion "borrows" beliefs that contradict each other from one, two, or more traditions. However it is positive when "borrowed" beliefs either compliment each other or are supplementary. For example, traditional religion places much emphasis on spiritual or faith healing. In fact, many independent churches are founded on this basis alone. Kimbanguism based in the Democratic Republic of Congo is a prime example.[5] Because

2. Mbiti, *Concepts of God in Africa*.
3. Ibid.
4. Bediako, "Understanding African Theology," 15.
5. Simon Kimbangu had a vision in which God instructed him to visit a certain sick person in the village and lay hands on her. He did just that and the patient was healed instantly. The word went out and masses started to follow him. Today there are

Simon Kimbangu emerged as a faith healer, just as Jesus of Nazareth, he gained a following which has now become one of Africa's largest independent churches.

Being a non-seminarian, Kimbangu's reading of the Bible, his hermeneutics, his liturgics, and even his administration is definitely heavily tinted with African cultural concepts of authority and mindset. When his followers call him "Father," the title has a double meaning. Sociologically, he is a family man properly respected as such. Spiritually, he is believed to be everyone's "father" also representing the heavenly Father. He is both fully spiritual and fully physical. The two natures are both attributed to him. Neither nature is viewed as secondary or inferior to the other. After all, it seems to be the nature of any religion to take on not only local color but also philosophical thought-forms of the new environment.

Across the board, African independent churches manifest both christological and cultural tendencies, and yet they uphold some basic concepts of God which are traceable to traditional religion. The various religious sectors of the Apostolic Faith are easily recognized by the attire worn by the adherents as well as the special Shepherd's staff carried by the leadership as well as by most male members. Most branches of this church practice polygamous marriages, like King Solomon or King David in the Old Testament. One thing is obvious about this movement. They are not bound by Western or mission-founded "ecclesiastical principles." Consequently, some of their concepts of God are drawn purely from either the Old Testament in general or African traditional religion, or both. Specifically, John the Baptist's attire is regarded as a symbol of being prophetic.

While concepts of God are not the essence of God, they are useful in expressing in human language what we otherwise could not communicate to others or pass on to younger generations. Over centuries traditional religion has developed its own concepts of God, which are necessarily couched in the people's culture. As a result there is a great diversity of perceptions of who God is on the continent and in diaspora. For this reason, we have devoted chapter four to the people of African descent who are not domiciled on the continent but share African concepts of God because wherever they are, belief in the one God, creator of the universe is obviously evident. Thus belief in God is one aspect that the

---

millions of Kimbanguists in the Democratic Republic of Congo (D.R.C.), in what was once Zaire.

African slaves in North America retained after they were bereft of their identity, dignity and language. African Christianity in diaspora and traditional religion wherever it is being practiced enjoy a common concept of God based on knowledge of the self-revealing God they worshipped. This similarity of the concept is largely dependent upon sustained cultural affinity and even identity.

If who God is were totally dependent on what we say about the Great Spirit, God would probably be nothing more than a fuzzy notion of reality named on the basis of mere human imagination. Fortunately that is not the case. African religion, which is the oldest form of monotheism,[6] has acknowledged and worshipped the one God, creator and ruler of the universe, who made divinity known to humanity. All the concepts of God discussed in this book reference us to this.

The God-talk and concepts described here are based on the premise that the Great Spirit referred to is the Unmoved Mover, the Uncreated Creator who sustains all creation. Note that these few chapters therefore do not seek to prove the existence of God. (This author cannot even imagine any existence without God's prior existence!) The task and focus here is a discussion of concepts of God from the point of view of select African sources including culture, traditional religion, philosophy, experience, revelation, and specific oral traditional sources like prayers, proverbs, songs, and the like. The book attempts to present concepts of God, the Great Spirit, in a language free from sexist and gender limitations since God is, in fact, beyond the limitations of the human language as previously noted. Furthermore, the author will use interchangeably the phrase "concepts of God" or refer to these collectively as "concept of God," just as one might talk about "African beliefs in God" or collectively "African belief in God."

Humans would have named God everything but who God is but God took the initiative to reveal who God is and that process is incessant. Every community has its local concepts of God; some concepts are the same as, or similar to, the biblical ones. However where such similarity occurs, it indicates universality, but where contrast is evident, that is due to the particularity of the revelation. Differently put, the historicity of the Incarnation is not to be confused with locality of divinity because God is both immanent and transcendent. Such instances only serve to reinforce the central concept of the universality of the one singular Divinity.

---

6. See chapter 2.

Therefore, the concept of God could not possibly be merely a figment of human imagination. Of the various theories of origin of religion, the ones that Africans least identify with are the materialist theories espoused by scholars like Sigmund Freud, Karl Marx, and Ludwig Feuerbach. God has made God's own sovereignty known to humanity. The materialist theories assume that humanity was groping in the dark as it were, so it had to create something called God. Concepts of God in African religion come from anything other than Feuerbach's personal objectification, Freud's illusion, or Marx's theory of religion as the opium of the people.

There are many who believe that God is God in spite of humanity's faith or unbelief. What encouraged me to write this book, despite the fact that the topic has been addressed by many from various angles, is that African religion, which founded monotheism, after decades of theological distortions by slavery, colonialism, and other forms of cultural invasion, is regrouping once more to give spiritual leadership to the world. Also, several of my seminary students, too many to name, kept pushing me to "share your African perspective of God with us!" Back in the 1980s the late Professor Dorothea Solle from Germany, a committed liberation theologian, put me on the spot as it were when she wrote this remark on one of my term papers at Union Theological Seminary; "we expect you to develop an African perspective of God as you have known this Great Spirit God in your culture."[7] At that time I viewed these as moments of inspiration, not compulsion. The experience now borders on being a "revelation" of sorts. On the other hand, my seminary students in African theological colleges and institutes were satisfied to hear me quote Paul Tillich's *Systematic Theology*, Karl Barth's *The Church Dogmatics*, or John Macquarrie's *Principles of Christian Theology*, depending on who wrote the prescribed textbook currently being used.

In this book the goal is to present a specific African concept of God. If the God who the church preaches and teaches in Africa, south of the Sahara, is the same that the traditionalists worshipped prior to the Christian and Moslem eras, let the reader draw any conclusions. The purpose here is not to compromise religious beliefs, but to present the African concept of the same God, wherever they may be.

I hope this study will probe deeper than mere comparison and reach the bedrock of African theology. While some of my colleagues prefer to

---

7. Dr. Dorothea Solle was a visiting professor of theology at Union Theological Seminary when I was a doctoral student there. Hailing from Germany, she taught liberation theology as well as the doctrine of God.

talk about African Christian theology, I simply refer to African theology. One major reason for taking this position is that theology cannot be done in a vacuum. In this case the context and matrix is African. I find it pointless to talk and reflect about God in terms of a "Christian" God and a "traditional" concept of God because God is God.

African theological concepts do not have to exclude biblical views of the divine as noted earlier since both traditions point to the one creator, God. Although there is an appreciable overlap in cultural expressions, certainly the Western perceptions of God cannot express African cultural presuppositions. Neither can African cultural expressions be expected to embrace all Western concepts of God. For example, to say "God is a great provider" triggers a more vibrant meaning to a community that confesses that it entirely depends on God's providence. Not every community that knows God, however, may acknowledge God as provider in this way. Some may know God as the great physician or something else. Knowledge of God can also connect many cultures. However, what is important is not so much what we know, as the value of our relationship with whom we know and what we have experienced. This is a critical criterion for any people of God who have experienced God as creator, provider, and savior. They not only know God, but also enjoy a relationship with the same. Thus, they celebrate, and give thanks, which is the essence of worship.

Concepts of God that evolve in this manner need not be controversial because the community's experience itself dictates and prescribes the desirable attributes. However, profusion of names, concepts and attributes can also legitimately create false impressions that there is a plurality of Gods. In African spirituality and God consciousness, there is only one God, creator and sustainer of the universe. This book will discuss this concept of God from various angles.

Chapter 2, "African Origins of Monotheism," serves the purpose of claiming that the idea of one God really started with African traditional religion in the people's response to the divine phenomena they experienced, including the divine revelation. On the basis of this, people responded by acknowledging the one and only creator and ruler of the universe. Among the various forms of monotheism, what was practiced by the Africans was apolitical yet moral and cognitive. It does not seek to impose itself on any other people as do Judaism and Christianity. Nor does it have any competition.

Chapter 3, "African Theological Concepts of God," constitutes the core of this book. It discusses various forms in which concepts of God are expressed. Discussion of good and evil occurs in the context of the one God; discussion of monotheism also obviously occurs in the context of the one God.

Chapter 4, "God Concept in African Diaspora," makes one major point that African concepts of God are so powerful that even when Africans were geographically displaced and dehumanized through the Atlantic slave trade, they managed to retain certain concepts of God that can still be traced back to the continent. Also implied in chapter 4 is the thought that African concepts of God have been and can be expressed by people of African descent through Black theology, liberation theology, as well as African theology.

Chapter 5 addresses the topic of the concept of God from the point of view that exonerates God from the presence of evil in a world created by a good God. It points out that, as far as African traditionalists are concerned, evil originates with creation, not the creator. It is a contradiction of terms to attribute the origin of evil to the origin and seat of holiness and goodness. Evil destroys but God creates. Chapter 5 is tied in to chapter 3 as are other chapters.

Chapter 6 concludes the book by expressing concepts of God theologically in order to ensure order and coherence. Chapters that might have described concepts of God in religious language benefit from the final chapter's theological approach.

two

AFRICAN ORIGINS OF MONOTHEISM

MONOTHEISM IS ONE PLATITUDINOUS characteristic of African belief in God. Defined as the doctrine that there is only one eternal God who is moral, just, merciful, omnipotent, omniscient, omnipresent, omnibenevolent, eternal, and transcendent, monotheism is central in the concept of God among various peoples of African descent, both at home and abroad. This chapter argues that, contrary to the general misconceptions about religion in Africa, monotheism originated there and is characteristic of the African concept of God, creator of the universe. The monotheism discussed here predates all others, including Hebrew, Christian, and Muslim monotheism. Based on sheer logic, Judaism, Christianity, and Islam are less than five thousand years old, whereas African religion, though not organized the same as these, is at least over ten thousand years old.

There are several types of monotheism. According to Jan Assmann, a renowned Egyptologist and author of *The Price of Monotheism*, "The monotheism of Akhenaten of Armana was a 'monotheism of knowledge,'" but Moses' monotheism was "a political monotheism, a monotheism that binds people together."[1] These two are distinct in that while the former belongs to the cognitive category, the latter is a matter of mutual obligation: the "I will be your God and you will be my people" type of covenant. Besides being younger, this type is limited to a people. Cognitive monotheism is knowledge of the universal God not limited to one people, but open to all. This type originates with God making God's self

---

1. Assmann, *Price of Monotheism*, 38.

known without any strings attached, as it were. This chapter argues that monotheism of knowledge originated in the African religiosity, which is why the term "African religion" in the singular is preferred over "African religions" in the plural. The implications have grave consequences. More specifically, a monotheism of African origins, as stated above, is belief in or worship of the one universal God but without a contractual covenant. Monotheism of African origin emanates from the very fact that God created the people whom God loves and the people respond in worship, praise and thanksgiving to the creator. African monotheism is not political, but is primarily relational—knowing God as one who created humanity. Therefore this is not an exclusive monotheism. Thus, African religion has never gone to war in the name of God as has been the case with Christianity and Islam. This is the umbrella under which all the concepts of God discussed in this book fall.

A REVELATION-BASED MONOTHEISM

Monotheism that originated in African religion was not conceived in contrast to polytheism or henotheism because, for the African, there was no other creator of the universe revealed to them. Regarding the general revelation by which God has made God's self known to various people throughout the earth, we agree with Dr. Idowu, who says, "there is no place, age, or generation which did not receive some form of revelation."[2] Since God has revealed divinity to every people including the African communities, it means the God they worship is the one living God, creator of the universe. A monotheism based on the creator's love is prior to a monotheism conceived following God's act of liberating the people of Israel. Put differently, God first revealed God's self as creator, then as one liberating the oppressed and suffering of the world. Granted, it is the same God. Here is the origin of monotheism, since the oldest remains of humanity have been discovered on the continent.[3] Furthermore, monotheism of knowledge is a result of God's own self-revelation as provider, sustainer, and one who saves. Thus, worshipping God was not a political or obligatory matter, but simply a response to the numinous, love, the providence.

2. Idowu, *African Traditional Religion*, 140.

3. Six million years old, found in the Tugen Hills of Kenya (Geisler, "Primitive Monotheism," 4).

Consequently, the monotheism of African origin is neither paternalistic nor parochial because the God they worship is for all—is the creator and sustainer of the universe. This is not a contractual monotheism. Theirs is not a monotheism that functions "as an organizing principle," nor is it some kind of a constructed "theological idealism." There are many facets to a discussion on a cognitive monotheism. In this chapter the discussion of monotheism as a characteristic of an African concept of God will draw from six select components: (1) names of God; (2) the attributes of God; (3) God and creation; (4) ancestorology; (5) God's "files" don't close; and (6) God, time and eternity. The criterion for the entire selection was African originality.

Dr. Norman L. Geisler, a prolific writer, profound thinker, and committed believer, is among scholars who have acknowledged and actually given credit to the so-called primitive religions as being, in fact, the original sources of monotheism. We cannot agree with him more when he says, "Contrary to popular belief, the primitive [sic] religions of Africa unanimously reveal an explicit monotheism."[4] Geisler's statement supports the views of indigenous African scholars, including Dr. John Mbiti, who, based on painstaking research throughout Africa south of the Sahara, observes that "in all these societies, without a single exception, people have a notion of God as the Supreme Being."[5] "Supreme Being" here is used synonymously with God. It is worthwhile mentioning that citing the Egyptian origins and Africa south of the Sahara, demonstrates how widely spread the concept is. Monotheism is literally spread across the entire continent, even though there was no single empire or media to connect these points. This again is the main difference and merit of cognitive monotheism which is not politically propelled. It is not imposed on any people. Nor is it in competition with any other since there is the only one God revealing divinity to all. I am persuaded to believe that human response to such revelation constitutes a major component of true religion. Cognitive monotheism recognizes God who was and still is the single universal and revealer of truth, ruler of the universe. It is neither legalistic, obligatory, nor exclusive. Cognitive monotheism has its roots in cognation.

4. Ibid.
5. Mbiti, *African Religions and Philosophy*.

EVOLUTION OR DEVOLUTION?

Human beings are challenged to keep the divine revelation and their response to it authentic. There are some theorists who advocate that revelation comes at the end of a series of religious forms. So they argue, monotheism is evolutionary, much the same as other biological systems. The other side argues for the devolutionary nature of humanity's response to divine revelation. The next few pages will discuss the two sides of the issue.

On the one hand, we have theorists like James Frazer, who contend that a monotheistic conception of God only evolved late in the history of religions. This would be a reasonable rationale coming from a scientist who believes in discovering knowledge and information. It therefore need not surprise us to hear the Frazer school of thought argue that religions evolved from fetishism to animism, and from this to polytheism and pantheism, or henotheism, and finally to monotheism. The manner in which Frazer develops his argument makes this theory quite plausible, although that does not necessarily make it true, especially when we take into consideration the issue of the uniqueness of the disciplines in question. Frazer is assuming that various theories of biological evolution are true even when there are not sufficient facts to support them, especially as it relates to things spiritual in general and specifically God's revelation.

On the other hand, in response to the Frazer school of thought, we may have to remind the advocates that religion is not always subject to scientific principles. In Assmann's words, "The truths of science may well, for the most part, be relative and have a limited life span, but that does not mean that they are compatible with everything else under the sun."[6] Assmann adds the critical observation that there are other disciplines which have "their own criteria of validity, verifiability, and falsifiability, which they are obliged to meet."[7] In agreement with Assmann, what Geisler cautions is instructive and conclusive: "Even if biological evolution were true on a biological level, there is no reason to believe evolution is true in the religious realm."[8]

After systematically challenging, and in fact, destroying the view from the Frazer school of thought, Geisler concludes that while it is

---

6. Assmann, *Price of Monotheism*, 13.
7. Ibid.
8. Geisler, "Primitive Monotheism," 4.

plausible that monotheism may have originated with the biblical account which states matters of origin: "In the beginning, God created the heavens and the earth" (Gen 1:1), giving the indication that there is only one God, hence the monotheistic concept, there is every evidence to believe that the first religion from which others devolved was the African primal religion. We have noted earlier that this was initially a cognitive monotheism, based on revealed knowledge prior to its eventual distortion. Luckily African religion has remained the world's first monotheism and has not devolved into polytheism, pantheism, animism or fetishism. Since often times evolution is response to the environment, it is fortunate that African religion has been surrounded by new monotheisms in Judaism, Christianity, and Islam, which, unfortunately want to usurp it of its birthright. We will not let this legacy go.

From our point of view, it is more plausible to conceive that it is when God's revelation is distorted that religion becomes polytheistic, or henotheistic, or even animistic or fetish, if not outright idolatrous or atheistic. While it is not unlikely that monotheism can be a result of a "culmination" of a long process that began with various forms of polytheism, it is more logical that religion begins as a pure religious response which eventually deteriorates. If religion was like democracy or capitalism or communism, one might expect it to evolve from animism to monotheism. But since African religion came into existence as a response to God's revelation, it can only have two options: either devolve into polytheism or pantheism or atheism, or remain constant as revealed.

However, it is a bifurcated process: (*a*) in ancient religions, henotheism "denoted a stage of religious development from polytheism to monotheism"; (*b*) monolatry is "a stage when monotheism disintegrates into polytheism."[9] Today, both henotheism and monolatry seem to mean more or less the same thing, namely, "the worship of a primary deity which allows for belief in the existence of others."[10] What we argue here is that African religion is the origin of cognitive monotheism in the broadest sense of the term . It originated with only the one creator of the universe with whom there was no competition or equal. In their respective original languages, the etymology of the numerous African names of God signifies singularity of God, the creator. The various names and attributes of God discussed here all point to this claim. Thus monotheism

---

9. Stuckenbruck, *Angel Veneration and Christology*, 17.
10. Ibid.

is the umbrella concept for all the African concepts of God discussed in this chapter (see the chart below).

Relative to the African origins of monotheism, James H. Breasted another Egyptologist, also describes the Egyptian origin of monotheism, rather than the biblical tradition. It can be argued that, since Moses' roots were Egyptian, that he was influenced there at an early stage cannot be ruled out. Breasted also indicates originality when he notes, "There was thus created for the first time a realm of universal values, and in conceiving the divine ruler of such a realm the Egyptians were moving on the road towards monotheism."[11] Breasted further documents the African origin of monotheism, noting "Through the concept of a great administrator and moral order, for which they had already created a word, the Egyptians might have advanced to full recognition of monotheism as later philosophers and theologians have done."[12] As a great nation, Egypt's influence spilled over to neighboring nations like Palestine and the Near East.[13] With the Egyptian background information, Geisler argues more persuasively that humanity's concept of monotheism has, over the centuries, "devolved, not evolved,"[14] resulting in several other versions of religions. To the present day, there are numerous schisms in the world of religions, thus manifesting the general human degenerative tendency. Roy L. Hales also supports Geisler in his observation that "there are many evidences of the loss of the original world monotheism, and descent into paganism."[15] Additionally, Hales notes that "the key early literate civilizations of Sumaria, Egypt, India, China and Mexico all show signs of having once been monotheistic."[16] Since Africa is among the oldest forms of civilization and is characterized by being notoriously religious, one can deduce that that religiosity was harnessed in a monotheistic sociopolitical milieu.

If we should judge a religion by its principles, rather than its adherents, it should be clear that monotheism is a major concept in African religion which is also the oldest religious civilization and culture. Since God is the creator whose spiritual presence is universal, many people of

---

11. Breasted, *Dawn of Conscience*, 145.
12. Ibid., 272.
13. Ibid., 23.
14. Geisler, "Primitive Monotheism," 5.
15. Hales, "Original World Monotheism."
16. Ibid.

African descent have always believed that the name God subdues and transcends all creation in heaven and on earth. If there are creatures above and beyond the universe, they too, are at God's disposal, and, of course, less than God since they owe their origin and existence to God. They may seem to be supernatural and may even be so on the hierarchy of creation but God is far greater, beyond measure or comparison. God is Supremo. The realization that no matter how great heavenly creatures may be, no matter how enormous some creatures of the sea may be, God is still greater, orients the African believers toward focusing their allegiance on God in the face of various technological, social and cultural challenges. All one has to establish is, is it a creature or God? If the answer is the latter, then the decision is made since there is only one God. Furthermore, it is amazing that Africans have never made any images of God, nor have they looked elsewhere for another God.

SINGULARITY OF DIVINITY AS BASIS FOR MONOTHEISM

There are some Eastern religions like Sikhism and a monotheistic Hinduism that subscribe to the idea of monotheism. By virtue of being an oral or non-literate religion, traditionalists express this singularity of divinity in proverbs and names of God which all signify singularity. While Islam is clear on this concept expressed in the term *tawhid*, African religiosity has always acknowledged Zimuyendayenda (the Transcendental God), even before the idea of the Ten Commandments was introduced by the Hebrews, or the Shahadah in Islam, which declares the tawhid. As noted earlier, here is a juxtaposition of the two distinct monotheisms, but the original is African with its nonpolitical and potentially transcendent character. In Judaism, the Shema also dictates the oneness of God: "Hear ye, O Israel, the Lord your God is One" (Deut 6:4). Since this is the same who initially revealed own divine identity and unity, we can now witness a diversity of monotheism. In this book, the argument is not that African monotheism is the only one. Rather, we argue that it is the *original* one. Its merit is that it is based on God's love for God's creation, to which humanity has responded.

SIX COMPONENTS OF AFRICAN MONOTHEISM

Since the African form of monotheism is the oldest and has an apolitical nature, what are the other components which make it unique, enduring and exemplary?

H. Wayne House makes a correct observation that among the people of African descent "monotheism of some sort, in which God is the eternal transcendent creator and sustainer of all things, is universally affirmed."[17] God is believed to be omnipresent, omnipotent, omniscient, holy, just, loving and merciful. Also in parts of Africa, some people teach that God, by virtue of God's own nature, is Unknowable. Most Africans do not desire to define God per se. They are contended knowing that God does exist, is real both in the mind and in reality. Also, God is invisible. However, other regions (from Botswana to Cameroon) know God as Nyame, while eastern regions, the Maasai of Kenya and Tanzania, call God Engai, meaning the Unseen, the Unknown. The Tenda of Guinea also call God Hounounga, meaning the Unknown. This does not mean they do not know that God exists. Rather it signifies that God is a mysterious reality.

But throughout the continent God is known as the Great Spirit, and consequently depictions of God are never permitted. Actually, in some areas, especially East Africa, African monotheism is so strict that God is thought of as uZivelele, meaning "the Self-Existent One."[18] Mbiti also reiterates that all African peoples consider God as creator. This is the commonest attribute of the works or activities of God.

The concept is expressed through saying directly that "God created all things, through giving him the name of Creator (or its equivalent), and through addressing him in prayer as the Creator or Maker."[19] Since all people of African descent acknowledge God as the Great Spirit, what praise names or attributes do they ascribe to God? Yes, God is known by various names but is one and the same, creator of the universe. The chart below has informative data that can be interpreted in a variety of ways. The countries covered here are what is generally meant by Africa south of the Sahara.

---

17. House, *Charts of World Religions*, 89.
18. Mbiti, *Concepts of God in Africa*, 89.
19. Ibid., 45.

1. Some African Names of God

Among most people of African descent, a name must have a meaning. Some countries have more than five names for God because of what they believe God has done and is, while others have only one or two. This might have something to do with the number of ethnic groups, and, or, major events attributed to God in the region. Here I have picked one name for God from each community and then list all the countries that use such a name. In some cases national boundaries do not coincide with language boundaries.

Name for God	African Countries Where Name Is Used
Mulungu	Zambia, Tanzania, Mozambique, Kenya, Malawi
Nzambi	Zambia, Rwanda, Burundi, Congo, Angola
Nyame	Cote D'Ivoire, Ghana, Zambia
Leza	Congo, Malawi, Zambia
Modimo/Molimo	Lesotho, South Africa, Botswana
Imana	Burundi, Rwanda

There are numerous names of God in Africa which are based on what God has revealed of God's own self to the people. Although there could not be one name for God on the continent due to linguistic differences, the most common throughout the continent include Nyame (Ghana), Nyadenga (Zimbabwe), Unkulunkulu (Zulu, South Africa), Olodumare (West Africa), Leza (East Africa), and Nzambi (Congo). We will revisit this section later.

2. Attributes of God

Attributes of God among the African people are really theological snippets. Like names, these are generated from what people observe about creation, or divine activities, or what they imagine about divine self-manifestation. Scholars generally classify these attributes into three categories: (1) eternal attributes, (2) intrinsic attributes, and (3) moral attributes. Let us now devote some time to a discussion of each of these as they pertain to African religiosity.

Countries that have the greatest number of names for God:

Country	Names for God	Total # of Names
Zambia	Chilenga, Chiuta, Lesa, Mulungu, Nyame, Nzambi, Tilo	7
Tanzania	Enkai, Ishwanga, Kyala, Kyumbi, Mulungu, Mungo, Ruwa	7
Uganda	Akuj, Jok, Katonda, Kibumba, Ori, Rugaba, Ruhanga, Weri	8
South Africa	Inkosi, Modimo, Mwari, Utixo, Raluvhimba, Ukulunkulu	6
Nigeria	Ondo, Chuku, Hinegha, Olodumare, Olorun, Osowo, Owo, Shoko	8
Congo	Nzambi, Akongo, Arebati, Djakomba, Katshonde, Kmvoum, Leza	7
Ethiopia	Tel, Yere, Siezi, Magano, Igziabher, Arumgimis	6
Ghana	Bore-Bore, Dzemawon, Mawu, Nyame, Onyankopon	5
Sudan	Ajok, Jok, Katonda, Ori, Rugaga, Ruhanga, Wari	7

A. Eternal Attributes

Eternal attributes make statements pertaining to God's timeless existence. Supreme among the attributes is that God is self-existent, which gives the connotation that God has always been. Moreover, no one or nothing caused God to come into existence, if there was a time when God was not, which, of course, there was not. Perhaps the very term God means just that—a being who has always been, is, and will always be. One of the Zulu names for God which expresses God's self-existence is uZivelele, meaning one who caused oneself to be, one who is of and in oneself. Aseity.

Self-existence also means God is independent; does not need anything or anyone to sustain divine being. In addition, Self-existence means more or less that God is perfect. Here, perfection means a total wholeness, not lacking anything, either directly or indirectly. Thus, when St. Anselm, Archbishop of Canterbury, defined God as "that than which nothing greater can be conceived," he was saying, in other words, God is Unknowable, or beyond finite comprehension. No one can completely understand God because of God's very nature. To say God is self-existent means God is the maker of everything that was made, but God own self was not made. Most people agree that this is the single highest compliment one can make about God. The self-existence of God implies originality, permanence, immortality, self-sufficiency, ageless, aseity, one who has always been. Like others, this attribute signifies God's oneness.

So, it is no wonder that most creation myths begin with the phrase "In the beginning, God . . ." They are affirming God's self-existence from before time. The Shona of Zimbabwe use three names for God (among others) all of which essentially refer to the same reality or phenomenon: *Muwanikwa, Mutangakugara, Chidzachepo (or Chidziwachopo)*. Each of these names means, if one were to translate them, "the one who was here or who existed first." Juxtaposed, the meanings of the three words sound like a riddle which we, as little boys growing up, used to challenge each other with. It went like this—who is the oldest among these three persons: one who was first to be in existence, or one who is everlasting in existence, or one who has always been in existence? The correct answer to all these was the same—any of the three. We will come back to this riddle later on in the chapter to go a little deeper into the language classification.

In chapter 3, we have discussed African names of God and explained how these three terms even allude to the concept of "monotheism." Other attributes under this present category include the First and Last, the Uncaused Cause, Spirit, Invisible, Invincible, Incomprehensible, Infinite, Everlasting, Immutable, and more. Whether the name expresses the via negativa or the via positiva, the meaning of the attribute is clear. What God revealed to the people of African descent is slightly different from the Christian understanding of God as far as these eternal attributes are concerned, assuming that Christianity incorporates the Old Testament revelation as well as the New Testament. Right through, there are attributes that clearly duplicate the biblical ones. But each attribute has its special nuances. Another set of attributes has to do with God's intrinsic nature.

B. Intrinsic Attributes

Intrinsic in this context means belonging to the very nature of God. So intrinsic attributes describe God's very nature, God's "genetic makeup," metaphorically speaking. God is characterized as omnipotent, meaning that God is all-powerful. This attribute has nothing to do with whether God can lift the heaviest rock or move mountains, which God himself created. It's not about muscular energy. Nor is it just a vain show of power. Omnipotence attributes to God sovereignty, free will, perfection, authority, a sense of finality. This attribute also refers to power purposefully and wisely applied. Power to control the universe, for example, or power to redirect the events in nature, to act at God's own divine pleasure, is described as omnipotence. Today many theologians and philosophers are asking if the all-powerful God can stop diseases like terminal cancer, for instance. Does this Almighty God have enough power to do anything? It is interesting that the same thinkers who ask these questions do not seem to realize that all-powerful also means power to do what God wants to do according to God's own free will. Not only does God have the power to not answer to curious souls that are trying to satisfy themselves that truly God is all-powerful, but God has the foreknowledge to address what is next.

God is also omniscient, which is the third attribute. There is nothing that God does not know, from an ant to an elephant bull; from the littlest entity to the hugest body on the face of the earth or under the oceans. Omniscience means *knowing everything*, but is not the same as foreknowledge, although there is a close similarity. The former is a state of knowledge including wisdom—of course, in God's case, we have to think in terms of perfect wisdom. The latter—foreknowledge—is knowing in advance what is going to transpire, or what will exist in the future, whether the near or the distant future. Where finite beings generally become aware of something, God already knows before the fact. Unlike humans, God does not become aware because everything exists in God's time and awareness. In God's omniscience, everything is in the present. Differently put, not only is omniscience an infinite state of knowledge, it is also wisdom. Close to the meaning of omnipresence is God's transcendence and immanence. These paradoxically complimentary attributes add on to the numinous nature of God. To put more weight on the one over against the other is losing the orthodox nature of God's intrinsic being. These couple of attributes almost foreshadow the two nature Christology which was only characteristic of Christ.

Like self-existence, no human being is ever given omniscience as an attribute, not even our geniuses. It is reserved for God only. There are sayings that substantiate or affirm God's existence in several cultural groups. For example, the Yoruba of Nigeria say, "Only God is wise"; the Akan of Ghana say of God, "He who knows or sees all"; in South Africa, the Zulu believe God is "the Wise One."[20] There are also numerous metaphors used to depict God's omniscience, but the most powerful one talks of God as "the big Eye." God is believed to keep "an eye" on every single thing in the universe, such that nothing escapes God's attention, as if escape were possible. The God who does not sleep or get weary of watching is the omniscient One.

Not only is God all-powerful and all-knowing, God's ability to know is comprehensive and perfect. Mbiti sums it all up by saying God "knows everything, observes everything, and hears everything, without limitation and without exception."[21] Omnipotence is one of the attributes of God throughout the continent and indeed the universe. Omnipresence means God is found everywhere—on the earth, in the sky, and under the seas and oceans. There is no place anyone can hide from the omnipresent God who is both transcendent and immanent.

Some cultures have likened God to a *great pool* of water, alluding to the presence of water everywhere. Or, when it rains every place gets wet. Actually the Karanga on the Zimbabwe and Zambia common boundaries have named God *Dzivaguru* (the Great Pool). Of course God is not everywhere just for the sake of being so. There is a purpose for the divine presence as well as omniscience and omnipotence all over the universe. Note that omnipresence is not synonymous with pantheism. The latter means God is synonymous with the universe and the universe is God without a personality. This is not the God acknowledged on the continent, because the African sense of omnipresence indicates God who has personality, though Spirit. So the Banyarwanda talk about God as a person when they say: "God who is met everywhere." This attribute clarifies

20. Ibid., 3.
21. Ibid., 5.

the misconception that African religion is animistic. In African religion there is a distinct difference between the vital force that permeates all nature and God. Because God is Spirit, "no one can make an image of him, nor can he be confined to space and time."[22] What we see from all these groups is a firm foundation of cognitive and moral monotheism. There is one moral God, creator of the universe. Even when the Lango people think of God as being "invisible but present, like the air and wind," they still conceive of a God who has personality. Additionally, when certain places are regarded as sacred because they are God's residence, such expressions only serve to help people to focus on God, but that does not take away divine omnipresence. Throughout these attributes, one cannot miss the commonness of ordinary people's knowledge about God. This personal God is not just an intellectual idea of God. God is transcendent and immanent.

Furthermore, that God is one is made obvious by the language of singularity with which God is made reference to. Indeed, God is a person to whom people feel they can talk, relate with and rely on in their daily affairs as well as in crisis situations when humanity is in danger of extinction. They turn to God because God is omnipotent, omnipresent and omniscient. Thus they have also identified other anthropomorphic attributes of God that indicate that God is moral. In fact, it is believed that in Africa, God is the guardian of morality as well as the highest standard of moral law. In African thought, God is the ultimate judge of all morals.

c. Moral Attributes

Moral attributes constitute the third category of the African attributes of God. These include the belief that God is good, just, merciful, faithful, holy, righteous, loving, kind and so on. All these attributes have been established on the basis of what the people have experienced in their encounter with this one God, creator of the universe. To say God is good is often an understatement because God is so benevolent to humanity that words can never fully express such goodness. The Bacongo say to a person who seems to be moody: "Rejoice, God never wrongs one." Incidentally this connects with the idea that God cannot be the source of evil because God is the source of goodness, righteousness and justice. The Akamba declare, "God does us no evil."

---

22. Ibid., 23.

With regard to the evidence of God's benevolence, the Kpelle people, according to Mbiti, "look at natural phenomena as indications of the goodness of God, and observe that 'He causes rain to pour down on our fields, and the sun to shine; because we see all these things of his, we say he is good.'"[23] Since departed spirits can be one of the most dreaded sources of evil, the Kagoro people believe that God is good because God protects them against the angered spirits of the departed, which they could not, otherwise, be able to deal with. To re-iterate, there is so much good that God does for the people that they do not ever see God being the source or creator of evil. To underscore the goodness of God, there is a Vugusu proverb which says: "What God offers you with one hand, you should take with both hands."[24] God is not only the giver of good things, but of good advice as well. According to Mbiti, "only goodness comes from him. So they pray for his help in hunting, warfare, and other undertakings. In his goodness he warns them, through sneezing, to refrain from murder, theft, and other evil deeds."[25] At the end of the day, all attributes give us more insight into God's eternal, intrinsic and moral nature and how God has been perceived by those who knew God before us. But common agreement lies in the acknowledgement that God is one, creator of the universe. Most African creation myths allude to this proposition. All these monotheistic expressions predate Judaism, Christianity, and Islam, which claim the front seats in monotheistic arena.

Myths about origins and a vast array of statements that attempt to postulate who God is, signify that there was when everything that is created did not exist. This gives nuances of a central control system. Furthermore, it is fairly evident that things that exist currently have not always been, neither will they last forever. Because they were brought into being, eventually they will cease to exist. Believing that God is the center for everything, is a major lesson from African monotheism.

This spiritual and intelligent Reality generally known as God at some point conceived and caused creation to come forth. The Rwandan sages teach "There is none equal to Imana [God]." Using the biblical image of God as the potter who single-handedly gives form to formlessness, it is believed that only the omniscient One molds a vessel from a chunk of clay. But beyond what the potter can do, God brings into being

---

23. Ibid., 35.
24. Ibid.
25. Ibid.

everything, including the clay, out of nothingness (*creatio ex nihilo*)! This process, from "nothingness" to "somethingness" (or creation), has been labeled many things over the centuries. But from the African spiritual point of view, we cannot conceive of a moral, omnipotent power or reality with the capability to intelligently design and create other than God, ruler of the universe. Throughout the discussion on attributes, one notes that reference to God signifies God's simplicity. Thus, various creation myths serve to explain that God is the only source of all existence. Since creation is closely related to the concept of monotheism in that there is absolutely no reason not only to acknowledge the creator but even worship the same, let us now discuss various creation myths with view to further confirm that Africa is the origin of monotheism.

3. God and Creation

Various African creation myths give us some idea of what the people believed about the origin of the universe. While the biblical tradition simply describes creation as a result of what God decreed, numerous traditional myths and several scientific schools of thought have explored other possibilities. Attempts to give scientific accounts some credibility have all been challenged to the point where no theory seems impeccable. For example, some thinkers attribute creation to the Big Bang, some simply call it "evolution," and a sector of the post-scientific age propose what they call "process." All these are attempts to describe the mighty work of intelligently bringing into being what was not—the transition from nothingness to tangible things, from one form of existence to another, or even from nonexistence to existence. Science as a discipline, by virtue of its own principles, cannot begin to deal with the concept of creation if this is understood to mean "bringing into existence that which did not exist prior." The principle that matter cannot be destroyed, nor can it be created, makes it difficult to discuss intelligently the subject of creation without being forced into a speculative evolution mode of thinking. Normally, evolution begins with "something" which then responds to its environment and does whatever is necessary or natural to adapt for survival. But the moment science follows this path, the scientists may have to account for what caused the existence in the first place. Gone are the days when some scientists argued for the spontaneous generation theory. If there must be a cause for maggots, there sure must be one for this intelligently designed Universe. A theist, along with a deist, would immediately name the prior cause God, whereas a non-theist and non-deist may attribute the occurrence to "chance," which is really a decent way to acknowledge ignorance of further information or explanation. I think that to believe in chance with regard to the creation of the universe that we know is really worse than a leap of faith.

Chance does not seem readily compatible or comparable to the character of the orderly Universe we observe. Furthermore, chance is not as scientific as scientists normally carry out their processes of deliberations. If it takes chance for someone to win the lottery, we also know that some would have played to win. So even chance is the second step. Regarding creation, there had to have been the Uncaused Cause which the scientist has not "discovered" yet since the cause is, in fact, not hidden, but revealed. Thus, the scientist may be looking in all the wrong places. African monotheism got it. Simple. God is creator. Uncaused cause and the created Universe are both known to us. However, we will need science to help us understand what all happened because science is good with analyzing, examining to learn what happened.

However, most of us respect science for the thorough job it does of studying analytically what the creator or chance has "brought into existence." This by no means signifies that science is not useful. The discipline of science plays a major role in discovering dates of origin, the nature of material (DNA), the texture, compound elements, mixtures, and behaviors of what was created. No other discipline has that capability, not even theology. The challenge of theology is to not only ascertain but possibly to name "who did it." Even if an atheist were to propose that "chance" did it, a theist would want to probe further to identify who or what caused and instituted the intrinsic nature that gave chance such capability. Science is very good at creating theories of "what might have happened"; theology tries to assign ownership or authority. African religiosity has simply named the creator of the universe and it attributes to the same anything that falls beyond human comprehension. Thus in this book we work with the "wager argument" that it is the creator who put the universe into existence and controls it. And so we seek to live in peace and harmony as the human race. If it turns out that the universe just got into existence by sheer chance, the African will not have lost anything, but gained peaceful existence. Thus, creation is attributed to the omniscient, omnipotent, and omnipresent one who takes an interest in the "work of his hands." There are not many myths that tell us about the origin of the creator because the story (myth) cannot even begin. To the contrary, most myths tell us what the creator brought into existence.

Manyuko is a Shona (Zimbabwe) term which attempts to accurately describe the concept of God as aseity. Though still metaphorical, *Manyuko*—translated (for lack of a better term) as "the sourceless source" or "the source of all sources"—means something whose intrinsic existence is bound in and of itself, and serves as the Cause of all existence before and yet-to-be. *Manyuko* is that First Uncaused Cause which itself has no time reference. In fact, to say "first" inadvertently misrepresents the nature of God because "first" gives the connotation that there was a time when there was nothing, which is not the case according to the theory or concept of *creation ex nihilo*.

Generally speaking, most creation myths seem to embrace this theory, as they all tend to begin with what God did in the beginning to bring into being humans, animals, even the universe itself. Several introductions to African creation myths render God as the agent of creation. For instance, (1) the Ekoi of southern Nigeria say, "In the beginning there were two gods, Obassi Osaw and Obassi Nsi. The two gods created everything together"; (2) the Dogon of Mali say, "At the beginning of time, Amma created the Earth and immediately joined with it"; (3) the Bantu of southern Africa say, "In the beginning, there was nothing but Nzame [God]"; (4) the Wahungwe of Zimbabwe say, "Maori created the first man, Mwuetsi"; and (5) the Zulu of South Africa say, "The Ancient One, known as Unkulunkulu, created everything." Further examples could be provided, but the point we are making is clear: God is the One who got it all started; so the Africans believe. Thus, God is conceived as *Manyuko*, because God is the author of "a beginningless and endless" existence—the Ancient of Days. No one or nothing causes God to come into existence. In everyday life, the term *Manyuko* signifies a surfacing of, for instance, water that was underground which all of a sudden emerges to the surface and begins to flow, forming a stream which never runs dry even in the dry season. *Manyuko* is a spring welling up to eternity.[26] One could think of *Manyuko* as mystery, but one could also begin to comprehend the meaning of "eternal God." All too often worshippers seem to underestimate the gravity of that opening phrase in many prayers: "Eternal God, creator of the universe . . ." It says it all. Back to the metaphor that is *Manyuko*.

---

26. John 4:1ff.

Normally, no one knows how far the water has travelled underground or whence it comes, before it gets to this point. Nor does anyone know the source. Interestingly enough, everyone knows that it is a spring but no one knows when it originated. Such origins are best described as mysterious yet real, known yet unknown. We have already discussed such a dichotomous nature in relation to God's attributes. To come to grips with all this, *Manyuko* is a metaphorical form of epistemology. To name God, the Shona have three terms which document for them God's eternal reality. They say God is *Mutangakugara* (one who got to sit first or one who got established first); *Muwanikwa* (one who was already there when others came later on, or one found already there); *Chidzachepo* (one who has always been there, or something immovable like a stump). Note that each term with the prefix "mu-" or "chi-" signifies singularity or unity of existence (oneness). As mentioned earlier, regarding the triple names that signify God's unicity regardless, in the Shona language classification "mu-" as in *munhu* means one person versus "va-" *vanhu*, many people; similarly, "chi-" versus "zvi-" singular versus plural. The point here is that all three names describe God as singular—hence monotheism based on God's presumed simplicity.

For African scholars, God's metaphorical and anthropological names, such as Excavator, Hewer, Carver, Creator, Originator, Inventor, and Architect, describe God as the great builder or excavator who created everything, one who alone created the World. Various designations point to God as, not only the One but also the omniscient, skilled, intelligent, moral and purposeful Being. Furthermore, these names emphasize God's position as the originator of all purposeful things. Mbiti is correct to say "every African people have a word for God and often other names which describe him."[27] For example, the Shona of Zimbabwe use the word "Mwari" ("mu-ari"), meaning one who is of and within oneself (aseity).

Various African names of God mean the one alone from whom all things derive their architectural origin, shape and existence. Mbiti also shares the view that God is here pictured as the architect of the universe, carving it with omniscient skill and artistry.[28] Collectively, African religion joins many traditions which believe that it is God alone who is the author of this life and beyond temporal existence! In African worldview,

---

27. Mbiti, *Prayers of African Religion*, Appendix A.
28. Mbiti, *Concepts of God in Africa*, 45.

existence takes two forms, spirit and physical, with the former outliving the latter.

4. God and the Ancestor Concept

As a spiritual phenomenon and manifestation, ancestorology is a paradigm for monotheism. Ancestor veneration is an inner circle and monotheism is the wider umbrella. Thus, ancestor veneration becomes an effective paradigm for commitment to the one and only Great Ancestor, God the creator of the universe. One would be remiss if one overlooked this very crucial spiritual discipline in African religion's concept of God. Ancestorology as a spiritual discipline teaches that no matter how great other people's ancestors are, *one remains faithful to one's own* because there is a relational and unconditional bond between them. Unlike the obligatory bond in Moses' political monotheism, the people of African descent uphold the oneness of God naturally, relationally, and rationally. Ancestorology activates this nonnegotiable creator-creation relational bond that exists between just the two: the creator and the creation, the spiritual and the physical. Even though there are several myths involving quarrels between the creator and the creature, still there remains a bond between them. In fact, the quarrels were often a result of betrayal of loyalty—loyalty to the One rather than the many. We have pointed out at the beginning of this chapter that African people did not have an option to be polytheistic or pantheistic since they began worshipping the one God who revealed God's self to them. Monotheism was the only reasonable and rational option. Using human images when talking about God is simply a pedagogical exercise to ensure human understanding of who God is. It has nothing to do with idolatry. Africans never worshipped idols, as noted above in this chapter.[29] Because the living dead served only as a channel to connect with the creator, death is a crucial state and stage in the life of an African. It is a turning point because life in God is eternal.

5. God's "Files" Don't Close

With regard to eternal life, when a patient dies in the physical sense, the medical system (hospital) generally closes the file (after collecting

29. Mbiti, *African Religions and Philosophy*, 44.

payment, of course). But it is not so with God, one of whose attributes is eternity. The individual's "file" is resumed at the spiritual level because spiritually speaking, the human being was created in God's image. So living with God eternally is one of the benefits and is Divine pleasure. Kwesi Dickson, who, in my opinion, is one of Africa's respected Old Testament scholars, is correct to say, "Indeed, it might be said that in African thought death leads into life."[30] Traditionalists maintain that at death they continue to exist in "God's file," an eternal spiritual state like God's, living in continuum with God. Thus, there is a distinct difference between medical science and African spirituality. The latter understands life as being in continuum with God, the Great Spirit and Creator. No wonder traditionalists also refer to God as Great Ancestor (however, this is beyond the categories of anthropology). Because Africans understand life to be in continuum with God, their monotheistic view leads them to ultimately seek the beatific vision. This beatific vision presupposes simplicity. One God, one Face.

For traditionalists, ancestorology—a mediatory channel or a form of spiritual hierarchy—is the means by which God is approached, a protocol signifying Africans' reverence to God. Contrary to popular misconception, rather than debilitate, in traditional religiosity, ancestors are believed to facilitate access to God. This was the only means traditionalists knew, but today both Christians and traditionalists also approach God through God. Incidentally, encountering God through God, or through one's ancestors, or one's savior, is one and the same thing, if, in fact, one has had a genuine religious experience. After all, if God revealed divinity to an African through spirit medium, it is appropriate for the individual to respond to God through a spiritual medium.

The concept of ancestors, which was grossly misinterpreted by those foreign to it, symbolizes a deep spirituality that could inform spirit Christology and Trinitarian spirituality. I agree with Dr. D. E. Idoniboye, a Nigerian philosopher, who pointed out that "the concept of the spirit in African metaphysics leads to a better understanding of the world around us."[31] If God who is Spirit is the First Cause, the Sustainer, the Alpha and Omega, then being in God's continuum is tantamount to eternity itself. So African people who knew God—the eternal God—before they heard

---

30. Dickson, *Theology in Africa*, 193.
31. Idoniboye, "Idea of an African Philosophy," 84.

about the resurrection that happens through Jesus, devised the ancestor concept which is a paradigm for eternal living.

Ancestors occupy a significant place in traditional religion because they are believed to possess supernatural powers. As they are strategically placed between the living and God the Great Ancestor, ancestors serve to point to the existence of the one Great Ancestor, God. As the guardians of morality, they work together with God (actually, God sends them to the living) to channel our lives so that the living are in God's continuum. Based on the hierarchy of ancestors, one can readily appreciate the monotheistic quality of African religion. Beginning with the youngest ancestors, going to the oldest or highest ranking ones, there are the immediate ancestors, beyond them are the distant ancestors, beyond these are the forgotten ancestors. The latter is the category believed to be so ancient that no one knows their names except the fact that they wield most power, and they are the closest to God. The title "forgotten" is ironic in that they are actually the ones the whole human system (the African community, that is) relies on. They are the ones who receive "instructions" or "blessings" from God and relay them down the channels to the living.

Although generally, the recipients thank the ancestors, or act as if they are actually worshipping their ancestors, the more spiritually mature people know that all blessings ultimately come from God. This has been an area of confusion and controversy regarding the source of blessings and who to acknowledge. When the living say their prayer to God, they do so reverently through the immediate and the distant and finally the "forgotten" ancestors who then deliver the prayer to God. This spiritual protocol has been grossly misconstrued to mean that traditionalists worship their ancestors, which is furthest from the truth. How could the founders of monotheism turn around and worship thousands of all the "ancestors" on the continent? Out of both ignorance and prejudice, Westerners called this channeling of prayers "round about or indirect," but technology can now enlighten everyone that any transmission must go through certain channels and that can happen instantly. In fact, the world of the computer which works through the air was patterned after ancestorology, or else there is a striking coincidence. All ancestors "forward" their peoples' requests to one and the same God, the Great Ancestor. Ancestors are also the custodians of morality in the tribe or community, just as God is the model for all morality in humanity.

Unifying morality among ancestors is consistent with that in humanity and God is the ultimate source of all morality. In the African context, there can never be ancestors who legislate a morality that is contrary to God's moral law as God is believed to be the source of all morality. This is primarily due to the fact of monotheistic African religiosity. Since we know that ancestors themselves worship God who they acknowledge as their creator in life and in death, it should not surprise us to see moral congruency. Universal morality does not only point to the universality of human conscience but also to the simplicity of the universal Divinity. Furthermore, as the living constantly seek communion with their ancestors, the former also seek communion not only with their fellow created members but with their creator who, in turn, desires to be in constant communion with all—both the living and the ancestors. For this and other reasons, it is a misnomer to refer to the ancestors as the "dead" unless this term is used co-terminously with "ontological metamorphosis." Life in God is a continuum. Furthermore, since God loves and cares for all creation, including the ancestors, divine love is not for the dead. Therefore there is no death in God's continuum. Ancestors live albeit a different morphology.

Africans who believe in life after this life are comfortable and at home in God's continuum. Traditionalists never mistook their forefathers and mothers for God because they knew that their mothers and fathers were and have always been creatures accountable to God who alone is Uncreated. Nor did they ever think of them as dead, or else they would not talk to them, revere them or seek to please them. As has already been pointed out, for a long time ancestor veneration has been mistaken for ancestor worship, especially by those who worship idols, or put God at par with idols.

6. God, Time, and Eternity

Everything that was created was created in time, but how did time itself come into being? Some how it seems time is an aspect of God's intrinsic nature. This is not to say God is time. No. Time itself was created by God but it has become an important matrix within which the universe was created and continues to unfold. The myths we discussed above all begin "in the beginning" signifying the importance of time. In time, creation will cease to be; but in God's continuum the ancestors will live eternally with God. Thus, while creation myths will transpire in the context of time, ancestors transcend time when they enter God's continuum.

The first point to note is that it does not appear prudent to permit our finite concept of time to stifle or limit our spiritual freedom to imagine the activities of God who is invincible, unknowable, self-revealing as well as eternal. Only God is not only initially eternal but is forever eternal. The rest, especially humanity, can only be eternal by God's invitation and divine grace. God reveals divinity because no creation can "discover" God unless such power has been granted by God own self.

Indeed, time itself was created. Prior to creation, time, in so far as God is eternal, might not have been a criterion or category for measuring anything. Furthermore, there was nothing to measure. Nor was there anyone wanting to calculate anything. Also, the concept of time itself expresses a component of finitude even when we talk about eternity because it is still an attempt to measure or calculate time! The limitation I am pointing out has already been demonstrated by the calendar system which describes time in terms of BCE and CE. Of course, before the calendar was invented by the Dogons of West Africa, there were other ways to compute time, but that only was created after the creation of day and night, according to the biblical account of how the universe came into being (Gen 1:1ff.). It seems to me that our time and language symbols are merely dots on God's drawing board with respect to the concept of eternity.

The problem of time is further compounded by the tradition of a linear mentality to which Africans did not traditionally subscribe. Numerical calendars are superseded by phenomenal calendars. In this state, "the events or phenomena which constitute time are reckoned or considered in their relation with one another and as they take place."[32] However, in discussing the concept of time among Africans, it seems Mbiti over exaggerated the matter when he said that Africans "have no concept of time." I would be more persuaded by the claim that theirs is a different type of chronometry. Even with the benefit of the clock or watch in present-day Africa, in a traditional setting, if an African says, "I will see you in the morning," morning ranges anywhere between 5:00 a.m. to 11:00 a.m. I think it is fair to say they have a greater tolerance of time. This is the tolerance that gives them the view, for instance, that "the eschaton" is not cataclysmic but instead it is conceptualized as unfolding

---

32. Mbiti, *African Religions and Philosophy*, 24.

gradually. "What is taking place now no doubt unfolds the future, but when an event has taken place, it is no longer in the future but in the present and past."[33]

The future cannot be isolated, because it is part of the past and the present. For example, let us say at 10:00 a.m. one says, "I will see you at 2:00 p.m." Is that not merely artificially *separating* time, which is not thinkable in the traditional concept of time? The traditionalist believes that 2:00 p.m. is already in continuum with 10:00 a.m. and the rest of the past, present, and future. It is believed that one cannot be unless one has been. And one who has been, is and will be. Thus, at any given moment in time, humanity is right in the middle of the time spectrum. This explains, at least in part, why traditional religion does not set out a time out there when one will "enter" eternal life. Eternity for anyone begins at the time when one becomes conscious of being in continuum with God who is the author and symbol of eternity. The community of ancestors is believed to be in that supernatural state of existence with God.

Regarding creation, what is important for Africans when thinking about the "beginning" of creation, is not getting preoccupied with time in terms of the calendar but visualizing creation as a phenomenon, and the creator's omnipotence, omniscience and omnipresence that transcends everything within the matrix of which the beginning eventuated. "God is seen as being in and beyond the "past."[34]

God of the "ancient of days" is the God of the present and the future, all of which are inseparable. Such consistence also underscores the concept of monotheism. God is one, past, present, and future. Overwhelmed with awe and amazement, one finds oneself without adequate vocabulary to describe such a numinous religious experience, so one simply says: how great Thou art! A component of the mystery or the creation phenomenon has to do with how the universe is such that it functions the way it does without the slightest human aid, and that no one knows really when it began except for the one who created it. Our scientists can always try to guess. This numinous reality which exudes authority and majesty is what grasps and spiritually dazzles most people's minds when they say "in the beginning." The point of departure for all creation myths, and perhaps the beginning of all theology, is located here. Even the Scriptures use this powerful phrase: "in the beginning." To say, "in the beginning,

---

33. Ibid., 23.
34. Ibid.

God . . ." summarizes all theology of creation. As already noted above, this is why all African myths of cosmology begin with "in the beginning."

In fact, "in the beginning," even as stated in the book of Genesis, refers more to God's greatness than to time. "In the beginning" is more a confession of faith than a scientific calculation of time. The statement undergirds phenomenon rather than chronology. For the traditionalist, time is merely an attempt to allocate eternity into "chunks" as it were; otherwise one has to deal with the whole spectrum each time one wants to refer to an event. Put differently, what human beings designate as time is a vain attempt to compartmentalize God's continuum. Human reason and imagination aided with revelation, helps to perceive God through God's own craftsmanship and aseity, through the written and spoken word as well as other phenomena granted by God. Time is within eternity, and eternity is within God, but God is above and beyond all.

three

AFRICAN THEOLOGICAL CONCEPTS OF GOD

PEOPLE OF AFRICAN ANCESTRY have an affinity toward the God who revealed divinity to them as their creator. Subsequently, they developed concepts of this God which reflect their cognation, expressed from their particular perspective. Two phenomena are prerequisite to the formation of concepts of God. First, God takes the initiative to reveal God's self to a people; second, the people either respond or do not respond. In the case of the people of African descent, they responded. This chapter recounts such acknowledgement in the form of theological concepts of God. Since there is a vast array of possible responses, it is not possible to exhaust the list here. We will only cite a few.

Since experience plays a major role in influencing one's perspective, attempts to seek answers to the people's economic, ontological, sociological, and spiritual concerns contributed to the development of their theological outlook in their respective regions. Owing to the cultural diversity on the continent, one can expect varying concepts of the same God. However, such diversity need not suggest plurality of divinity. Thus, a critical reflection on the African perceptions of who and what God is (as that is being constantly revealed to the people in various circumstances) is informative and necessary in any endeavor to construct a coherent theological concept of God.

This can be an ongoing process because God continues to be. What God is doing constitutes a major component of what elements characterize the proper subject of theology. However, not all theological utterances are to be regarded as instructive statements that ought to be featured on God. Divine manifestations are the bases upon which the concepts may be conceived and constructed. How any God-related data is interpreted depends on the community's experience, spiritual orientation and religiosity. Word of caution, since theology does not determine divine actions, neither does it discover a hidden God if God were to hide, it can only be the people's reflection on divine acts in the world and the articulation of such reflection. Put differently, it is a literary form or expression of the people's experience.

Against this backdrop, one attempts to articulate concepts of God from an African perspective, in spite of cultural diversity. In addition, based on a common spirituality, an African American concept of God is included in this book for two reasons: first, to show that these concepts are part of the African wherever the people of African descent may be domiciled; secondly, to demonstrate that the God worshipped in Africa is not just a local divinity but universal and, in fact, the living God believed to be acting in history as Black liberation theology claims. So, chapter four will resume discussion in this chapter as both a carry-over and an adaptation of God concepts on the continent.

What Africans know about God was revealed to them in one form or another by the Great Spirit Being. Human reason may serve to receive and reflect upon the revelation, albeit critically, but does not have the prerogative to create concepts of God *out of nothing*. Concepts about God discussed here are not so much what the people figure out as what God chooses to let them know through apprehending the divine revelation. Since God's acuity is inexhaustible, attempts to define divinity often fall short of the wholeness of God. Fortunately, in African thought, that finitude is a further attribute of the people's knowledge of who God is.

DARING TO DEFINE GOD

A definition of the subject matter at the outset is necessary for a more meaningful discussion of the concept of God. With reference to this chapter, God is that spiritual reality which is not only greater than any human reason can conceive, but sustains everything that constitutes the universe and beyond. God is Reality without a beginning or an end, as expressed in several eternal attributes. Many thinkers concur with the view that God cannot be defined in terms of time, space, quantity, or volume, since all these categories were brought into existence by God and are not suitable instruments to figure God. God is *Wholly Other*. God is *God*.

The Shona of Zimbabwe have characterized this Spiritual Reality as *Zimuyendayenda*, meaning a vast eternal reality that transcends all and is not only immanent, or invincible, or immutable but forever eventual. One could state attributes that are via negative, but still that would not say everything about God. When St. Anselm (1033–1109), who is counted among the world's greatest philosopher-theologians, made a tremendous contribution to Western philosophy and theology by offering a definition of God, he still did not explain who God *is*. All he succeeded in doing was to say what God is not. To say God is "that than which nothing greater can be conceived" does not define God any differently than does one of the African attributes of God that describes the creator as the Unknowable.

Africans who are the originators of monotheism as discussed in the previous chapter, were already worshiping God who had revealed eternal divinity to them when Euro-Americans were still holding philosophical debates about whether or not God exists. Many serious thinkers admit that the conclusion the Westerners arrived at by employing the five classical proofs of the existence of God was based only on rationality and so possibly is discontinuous with what the Africans discerned primarily through experiencing the revelation in addition to their rational thinking. However, since God reveals divine glory to God's people everywhere and for a purpose best known to God's own self, one could concede that both Westerners and Africans, not excluding the Asians, may have received the revelation at various times. The differentia comes from how the respective peoples responded to the numina. At best, Anselm's statement only gives a hint of who God is. By indicating who God is, Anselm's definition does what most definitions normally accomplish. However, with reference to God, it leaves much to be desired. The predicate is simply an indication, not a precise designation. One can only say his was a tremendous contribution toward the task before theological scholarship.

Given their affinity towards things spiritual, Africans learned to approach the realm of God who is spirit, in a relational manner, and without doubting that they were in the real presence of the Great Spirit. Approaching God in spirit means that the people are spiritually oriented such that when God reveals divinity, a positive response is forthcoming. So, to say God is spirit is, to the traditionalist, synonymous with an affirmation of God's reality or unquestionable existence. For a people who have an affinity for the spirit, response to the Great Spirit is like their second nature. We noted earlier that Africans acquired their awareness of God primarily experientially and also cognitively. Aware of the "omnipresence" of their ancestors, Africans know that the creator can be both immanent and transcendent at once because that was their experience of the ancestors. In this regard, ancestorology is, for the African, a useful theological paradigm. Furthermore, such universality is concrete. In sum, God's intrinsic nature, moral character, and eternal being inform and influence the conceptualization of God in African religiosity.

THE NATURE OF GOD

All concepts of God are an attempt to name and describe God's nature as gleaned from various divine manifestations. From the local to regions, God's nature is discerned from God's activities such as revelation. Some attributes necessarily imply more than what the people may have verified because they happen sporadically.

One of the commonest attributes is that God is omniscient. God knows everything because everything, including potentiality, was created by God. This attribute is reflected in God's names, such as Olodumare, Chuku, Nyame in West African regions; Nyadenga or Mwari in Zimbabwe; Unkulunkulu, uZivelele, Modimo, or Inkosi in regions within South Africa; Mulungu, Engai, and Leza in East African regions; and Nzambi in Central African regions of Congo, Burundi, and Uganda. These numerous names of God are based on what God has revealed about own self to the people. In spite of the fact that there could not be one name for God on the continent due to vast linguistic variety, there is amazing theological congruity in the meaning of such names. This points to the fact that indeed the referent is essentially the same, hence the origin of monotheism.

In addition to divine omniscience, God has foreknowledge. The former refers to knowing everything, while the latter means knowing what will transpire before it ever happens, without having caused it to happen. Neither of these terms is synonymous with predestination. Where finite beings generally become aware of something, God already knows before the fact. Unlike humans, God does not become aware because everything exists in the present in God's time and awareness. Omniscience is infinite state of wisdom and knowledge. It is no wonder traditionalists always turn to God for wisdom in times of crisis. Regarding views on predestination, various ethnic groups hold similar perspectives. "The Yoruba believe that a man's doings on earth have been predestined by God."[1] To heighten the drama, they believe that "before a person is born, he stands before God in order to choose, receive, or have his destiny affixed to him."[2] However for the African, predestination is a positive attribute because it pertains only to knowing the outcome, rather than putting people in undesirable circumstances such as depravity. There is a thin line between predestination and foreknowledge. Given their positive attributes of God, what God set up for God's own creation is best for the same. There could be nothing better. A proverb that endorses the belief in predestination says: "If God serves you rice in a basket, do not ask for soup."

For everybody, God is the origin and destination of human life. According to this thinking, the implication is that human souls existed prior to coming into the physical world where they dwell for up to several decades, then will have to return where they originated. Believing that recovering from illness or dying is all in God's hands, the Lugbara say, "If God wants him to die, then truly he will die. If God wants him to recover, then truly he will recover."[3] Another ethnic group, the Toposa, simply summarizes it all in its view that "God determines the length of every person's life on earth."[4] Apparently, according to this worldview, whether we live or to die is all God's prerogative, because God is the author of life, the beginning and finisher of life. This concept is the basis for several others which emphasize the I-Thou relation. God is a Person whom humanity relates to and relies on for day to day survival. God has what it takes for humanity to be in existence, both in the spirit and in the physical states, in life and in death, which is why there can be no hell in the African worldview.

Also, because God is omnipotent, life and death are all under divine control. To explain why calamities can happen even though God who is good, almighty and loving is in charge, the Balese believe that "God is surrounded by two spirits. One of these spirits is God's son who knows all the thoughts of God, and decides for the good or ill of men in the world."[5] This theologically fine distinction serves to exonerate God from ever being associated with the cause of evil in a world created by

1. Mbiti, *Concepts of God in Africa*, 53.
2. Ibid.
3. Ibid.
4. Ibid., 55.
5. Ibid., 54.

a good, omniscient, and omnipotent God. Although this happens with God's knowledge, not everything that occurs has God's sanction. This, however, does not mean God is any less omniscient or omnipotent. Also, the Balese concept alludes to the idea of a demi-god which we will not expand on here.

Furthermore, understood from an African perspective, omnipotence is not sheer flexing of power for its own sake. Rather, it refers to power purposefully and intelligently meted out as God did in the creation of the universe, or in designing a simple insect like a mosquito. Power to control the universe is the meaning of all-powerful, all-mighty, and all-knowing. Because God has the power and authority even to redirect the events in nature, some theologians and philosophers today are asking why the all-powerful God will not stop terminal cancer or any of these devastating killer diseases. Does this almighty God care to do something about the human plight? Under what circumstances does God apply divine omnipotence? Apparently omnipotence also means that God chooses what is purposeful according to God's own judgment and morality. The African approach to God's attribute of omnipotence leaves everything to God's pleasure. In fact, when they are confronted with a mammoth task, they generally surrender everything to God: "Leave it with the creator who is all-wise." This in itself is African wisdom, and it's far from "ignorance is bliss" complex. Anyone who presumes to have more wisdom than God is, in fact, more ignorant than one who concedes that God is all-wise, and what that entails.

As an attribute, omniscience is reserved for God only. Several ethnic groups substantiate this. For example, the Yoruba of Nigeria say, "Only God is wise"; the Akan of Ghana say of God, "He who knows or sees all"; in South Africa, the Zulu believe that God is "the Wise One."[6] There are also numerous metaphors used to depict God's omniscience, but the most powerful metaphor is one that refers to God as "the big Eye." God is believed to keep "an eye" on every single thing in the universe. Nothing escapes God's notice. The omniscient One does not sleep or get weary of watching. Not only is God all-knowing, God's ability to know is comprehensive and perfect. Mbiti sums it all up by saying God "knows everything, observes everything, and hears everything, without limitation and without exception."[7] Well said. However, the problem arises when

6. Ibid., 3.
7. Ibid., 5.

questions relating to what God is doing about the situation are raised. For the African it gives the peace of mind to believe that God knows, since God is caring, just and merciful. God will intervene.

Indeed, throughout the universe, omnipotence is one of the attributes of God. Coupled with this is God's omnipresence. In God's transcendence, divine sovereignty is evident everywhere in the universe. There is no place anyone can hide away from the omnipresent one who is also simultaneously all-knowing. Some cultures have likened God to a great pool, alluding to water which, when it rains, makes every place wet. Actually the Karanga of Zimbabwe and Zambia have named God *Dzivaguru*, meaning the Great Pool. Of course, God is not everywhere just for the sake of being so, even though omnipresence is part of God's intrinsic character. There is a purpose for the divine omnipresence as well as omniscience and omnipotence. Teleology informs the people's existential theology. Through human reason, many have come to the conclusion that the all-wise God always does things for a purpose.

The African concept of divine omnipresence is not synonymous with pantheism because God is not coterminous with the universe. The Universe is God's creation, which is separate from the creator. A pantheistic god is not the one who is acknowledged on the continent. Furthermore, the African sense of omnipotence indicates God as a person, though Spirit. So the Kono anthropomorphize God when they say, "the One you meet everywhere,"[8] thus clarifying the gross misconception "that African religions are animistic." First, there is only the one God; second, there is only one African religion—one people, one religion, one God. Furthermore, this sheds some light on the African concept of God. What we see from all these groups are remnants of cognitive and moral monotheism.

There is one moral God, creator of the universe. Even when the Lango think of God as being "invisible but present, like the air and wind," they still give God a personality. Combining divinity and humanity, the Kurama believe that "the departed constitute, as it were, the ear of God, so that through them he can hear what the living are doing or saying."[9] Since the ancestors are regarded as the guardians of morality and God is the standard for morality, God and the ancestors share the task of being guardians of morality. And, since the living depend on both powers, it is

8. Ibid.
9. Ibid., 4.

in obedience to these that their survival depends on. In short, the physical world must be in harmony with the spiritual world, and vice versa. This is the formula for a truly abundant life.

Reference to God's residence is one more metaphor for divine humanity. So, certain places may be designated as sacred because they are regarded as God's residence. Such expressions only serve to help people focus on God. The language of locality, particularity, and specificity does not take away the quality and effectiveness of divine omnipresence. Throughout these attributes, one cannot miss the commonness of ordinary people's knowledge about God precisely because God is "everywhere"—immanent and transcendent, compassionate and immutable, merciful and invincible. This personal God is not just the African people's theological idea of God; rather it is a self-revealing God theologized. For them, more than just a concept, God is real. Furthermore, the simplicity of God is made obvious by the language of singularity with which God is made reference to. Indeed, God is a person with whom people feel they can talk, relate and rely on in their daily affairs as well as in crisis situations when humanity is in danger of extinction. They turn to God not only because God is omnipotent, omnipresent and omniscient but because they have also identified God's moral attributes albeit divine simplicity.

In creating moral attributes, the people believe that that is what God's nature is, based on what they have experienced through sporadic instances of divine revelation and providence. In conceiving God as all-powerful, it is inconceivable that God can have any adversary because, besides being almighty and all-wise, God is the ultimate. Although the term "supreme being" was used by the early Western anthropologists and even missionaries in a sort of derogatory sense, to designate a god who was exclusively for the Africans, most people of African ancestry believe that God is just that: Supreme Being, (Olodumare, Unkulunkulu, Nyadenga, Inkosi, Modimo, Mulungu). All these names point to divine insuperability. On a hierarchy of beings, God is ranked highest by any criterion. So, when attributes of God ascribe ultimateness, that in itself is an added quality which does not have an adequately descriptive name, except to say the Unknowable.

Thus, to say God is Unknowable need not suggest the absence of revelation because there is adequate occurrence of this. Nor should it give any semblance of ignorance. To the contrary, from an African epistemological criterion which acknowledges that not to know is knowledge in itself, one of the characteristics of God's intrinsic nature is that divinity is Unknowable. After all, knowing God does not cause God to do for humanity what God would not will to do in God's own freedom and will. The reason God revealed divinity to humanity is not only because the latter had no way to comprehend the former, but also in order that humanity might know the divine purpose of creation. Put differently, the creature does not know its creator unless the creator makes own self known. Consequently, all African concepts of God weave in and out of the revelation, not divination or imagination.

Omnibenevolent suggests that people have experienced that God is the ultimate provider for all their essential needs like the rain, the harvest, good health, children, and indeed life itself. Since a relationship with God is inseparable from survival, God is believed to be caring, loving, just and moral among other attributes. Hence several moral attributes have been developed such as goodness, justice, mercy, compassionate, loving, holy and more.

But holiness is one attribute that sets God, the creator, apart from all that was created. Viewed as wholly other, God is not only elevated above all creation but also exonerated of sin, failure, unrighteousness, and wrongdoing. One ethnic group says, "God cannot be charged with an offence." The Ila show in their attitude that "God is holy."[10] In addition to these, Mbiti lists other ethnic groups that also share a sense of God's holiness. Many believe that "the sacrificial animal must be of a solid color and without blemish. This is a symbol of holiness."[11] Perfection symbolizes holiness.

Mbiti may be correct to say the word *holy* is not found in many African languages, "but the concept is not lacking" because among the Shona, the concept of holiness or sacredness is prevalent. The word *Kuera, or kueresa,* means to be holy *and* to make holy, respectively. A thing can be said to be sacred or holy. The Shona actually have a day of the week set apart as *chisi,* a holy day when working in the fields is forbidden. Those who do go into the fields can be sure that they will suffer dire consequences sooner or later. Hence the saying *chisi hachieri musi wechinorimwa* (meaning if one does not observe this *chisi,* one will eventually suffer great adversity).[12] The culprit will be punished, not only by

---

10. Ibid., 41.
11. Ibid.
12. This saying was first told to me by my father, Sekuru Haadi Muzorewa.

the community, but by the ancestors who also wield supernatural power. In each case, one can be sure that the punishment is commensurate with the magnitude of the disobedience. Incidentally, necessary adjustment is made between punishment for a person who violated *chisi* inadvertently and one who just dared the powers that be. For the former, punishment takes the form of a warning. Justice is another aspect of God's holiness. Muzorewa notes that "in traditional life God is believed to intervene on certain occasions for the purpose of preserving justice."[13]

That God is compassionate and merciful is a truism among various ethnic groups. Almost invariably, when a recovering patient says, "If God were not the God of mercy, I would not be talking with you now," you know that the person nearly died.[14] But what is clearly suggested is that human beings live by God's mercy. An elderly person, among the Akamba, may say, "Oh, how profoundly merciful God is"[15] when he or she has observed circumstances that were beyond human control yet turned out to be non-life-threatening. But for the Chagga people, Mbiti adds, "Not only is God merciful. He [sic] is also tolerant." All these sayings are various ways of expressing God's anthropomorphic as well as moral attributes. Mbiti writes, "The pity of God manifests itself in terms of comfort to his [sic] people when they are in distress."[16]

Assigning these human attributes to God also suggests that people have a sense of reciprocity with God just as they have with fellow human beings. Among the Shona is this proverb: *kandiro kanoenda kunobva kamwe*, which is more or less equivalent to "one good turn deserves another." Reciprocity and accountability regarding human response to a neighbor, triggers a comparable obligation to God. In addition to the moral attributes is a category of eternal attributes which indicate the people's sense of time regarding existence, reality and posterity.

Unlike the moral attributes, eternal outweigh any qualities a human may exhibit. They are exclusive to God. Since these eternal attributes describe God, the African people therefore associate God with the realm of heaven or the skies. Some traditional names that reflect this quality are *chidza chepo* (the Pool), *muwanikwa, mutanga kugara* (the Riddle). This Trinitarian designation may suggest that God does not change no

---

13. Muzorewa, *Origins and Developments of African Theology*, 10.
14. Mbiti, *Concepts of God in Africa*, 30.
15. Ibid.
16. Ibid., 34.

matter by what name people may call God. Regarding God's invisibility, Spirit and incomprehensible nature, the Moru people believe "that it is the spirit of God which empowers the rainmakers to 'produce rain' and perform other duties."[17] What is true of the rainmakers is also true of the traditional healers. Their power to cause it to rain or to cause healing to occur is not their own. God gives it to them. The Akamba say, "God is the most superior Physician."[18] All prayers for the sick no matter how they are channeled, ultimately end up at God's throne. The Vugusu "reaffirm their belief in God's healing work through praying every morning, asking him [sic] to 'spit' upon them his all-powerful medicine, to heal and prevent illness."[19] No wonder most traditional healers do not charge a fee for healing their patients. They believe that the knowledge and power to heal is a gift from the creator, to whom belongs all glory and honor. If a patient dies in spite of such prayers, the conclusion is that it is God's will, for all life belongs to God. That God saves is central in most ethnic groups. For instance, the Abaluyia's name for God can be translated as "One who saves, helps, or steers."[20] Two of the Barundi names for God mean "There is a savior" and "Only he [sic] can keep our lives."[21]

Regarding the relationship between humanity, the spirit world and God in matters of health, like healing, we agree with the Burkina Faso scholar Dr. Malidoma Patrice Some that "because healing in the indigenous world includes the dimension of the Spirit, definitions of illness extend also to the unseen worlds of mind and Spirit."[22] Although many illnesses are genuinely physiological, the majority of cases are psychosomatic disorders.

Many scholars observe that African culture is akin to Jewish culture, and consequently there are points of great similarity. For instance, the Jewish faith-healer who simply said, "Daughter, your faith has healed you; go in peace" (Luke 8:48), healed by channeling God's healing power. Also, when Jesus instructed the patient he had just healed to "sin no more," he meant that the person should be positively connected with the rest of the spirit-world, and not be bound by the evil spirit. In another

17. Ibid., 24.
18. Ibid., 68.
19. Ibid.
20. Ibid.
21. Ibid.
22. Some, *Healing Wisdom of Africa*, 29.

episode, when Jesus raised a dead young man just by touching the coffin and saying, "Young man, I say to you get up" (Luke 7:14), the onlookers remarked, "God has come to help his [sic] people" (7:16).

Another point of contact is that all these wonderful acts were possible because Jesus, the *homwe* (the repository), was without sin.[23] We further concur that because God is holy, "the person into whom his [sic] spirit enters is thought to acquire a certain degree of holiness and is consequently regarded as ritually 'dangerous.'"[24] Thus, God is believed to actually take possession of the *homwe*, a select individual. The *homwe* among the *Shona* is selected for the purpose of conveying salvific acts in history. Again, one cannot emphasize enough that it is absolutely necessary that the *homwe* be holy and without blemish as God is holy. Holiness seems to also relate closely to eternity since it is characterized by the absence of evil.

Pertaining to God's eternity, self-existence gives the connotation that God has always been. Moreover, no one or nothing caused God to come into existence if there was a time when God was not, which, of course, there was not. Perhaps the very term God means just that, that this is a Being who is and has always been. For God there is no such thing as the future because God is from everlasting to everlasting; God is The First and Last.

Self-existence also means God is independent and does not need anything or anyone to sustain divine being; it means more or less that God is perfect. Here, perfection means a total wholeness, not lacking anything, either directly or indirectly. Thus when St. Anselm defined God as "that than which nothing greater can be conceived," he was saying in other words that God is unknowable. No one can completely comprehend God because of God's very nature. To say God is self-existent means that God is the maker of everything that was made, but God own self was not made. This is the single highest compliment one can make about God. Finally, self-existence of God suggests originality, permanence, immortality, self-sufficiency, one who has always been and will forever be, thus divine eternity.

What then is the meaning of time with reference to God? When all the creation myths begin with the phrase "In the beginning, God . . ." they are affirming God's self-existence from time immemorial. The

23. Heb 4:15; 1 Pet 3:18.
24. Mbiti, *Concepts of God in Africa*, 4.

Shona of Zimbabwe use three names for God (among others), all of which essentially refer to the same reality or phenomenon: *muwanikwa, mutangakugara, chidza chepo*. Each of these words means, if one were to translate them, the one who was here or the one who existed first. Juxtaposed, the meaning of the three words sounds like a riddle. Elsewhere, we have discussed African names of God and explained how these three terms even allude to the concept of "monotheism."

SELECT CONCEPTS OF GOD AND ORAL SCRIPTURES

In conclusion, African concepts of God are well established through the people's religious beliefs. Top of the list is the concept of the one God. Africans have always believed in the one God. Although God is one, various ethnic groups name the same reality according to their respective languages and religious experiences. Belief in one God makes African theology a monotheistic, theo-centric theology. As such the African origin of monotheism is actually grounded in theology proper.

One of the most common concepts of God in African cultures points to God as the creator. Thus African theology is a particular form of a creationist theology. African religious belief is the basis for creationist theology because the people believe that it is God who brought all creation into existence. No wonder one of the Shona (African) names for God is *musikavanhu* (creator of humanity). African creationism is actually the opposite of Darwinism or the Big Bang theory. Like biblical theology, African creationism subscribes to the *creation ex nihilo* theology. God is Alpha and Omega, the Beginning and the End. All creation myths indicate that it all started with God. It is God who separated the waters from the land, the skies from the earth, day from darkness, and so forth.

Another concept of God of great significance is anthropological. God is the Great Ancestor. Giving God human features, Africans view the divinity as the most powerful, caring, able spiritual parent who exists in the Spirit. This means at the end of physical existence, all souls will return to this Great Ancestor, while flesh returns to dust. For African religion creationism is not literal. It is practical.

The nature of God as conceived by most Africans is that of a transcendent Being who is also immanent. Because God is self existent, omnipotent, omnipresent, omniscient, and omnibenevolent, traditional religion qualifies to be classified as a monotheistic religion, which is its ultimate concept of God.

This traditional of God concepts has been preserved by and passed down the generations through oral texts, like proverbs and other oral educational forms of wisdom. Below are several proverbs that are commonly used to teach young generations who God is and how God is such a central power in the community. The chart with "wisdom literature" is also another means of instruction. It is of course understood that wisdom comes from God. In my other book, I have discussed at length the importance of these proverbs for sources of African theology.

God-Proverbs

Proverb	People
God saves the afflicted according to his will.	Ganda
God gives his gifts to whomsoever he favors.	Ganda
God does not speak to anything; if he should speak to anything, the world has come to an end.	Lozi
What God puts in stone for someone never goes rotten.	Ganda
The plant protected by God is never hurt by the wind.	Banyarwanda
God goes above any shield.	
Better become lame through God's aid, than die.	Ganda
Man is a speaker; God is the Answerer.	Bacongo
The enemy prepares a grave, but God prepares you a way of escape.	Banyarwanda
God is greater than an army [of enemies].	Barundi
Rather than praise yourself, let God praise you.	Banyarwanda
The creature is not greater than its creator.	Barundi
God knows the things of tomorrow.	Barundi
To him to whom God gives, he does not give by measure.	Barundi
If God dishes your rice in a basket, do not wish to eat soup.	
No one can take from him to whom God has given.	Barundi

Wisdom-Proverbs

Proverb	People
I pointed out to you the stars and all you saw was the tip of my finger.	Sukuma
The unfortunate cow has to stay outside in the rain while the dog stays inside the house at the fireplace.	Sukuma
Wisdom is like a baobab tree—a single person's hand cannot embrace it.	Akan/Ewe
When elephants fight, the grass gets hurt.	East Africa
The cooking pots of many are broken.	Ganda
One who keeps saying, "I will listen [obey]" will be cooked with the corn cob.	
Giving is not losing; it is keeping for tomorrow.	Lozi
When a child is well-fed, he looks upon a grave as an ordinary heap of earth.	
When a big tree falls, the birds in it scatter.	
The sounds of a person's cry show his tribe.	
If a frog has no belly when it is young, what will it have when it is old?	
If an old woman says that she was once beautiful, you can verify it from the back of her neck.	
The hen with chicks does not swallow the worm.	
To lose the way is to learn the way.	

four

GOD CONCEPT IN AFRICAN DIASPORA

PEOPLE OF AFRICAN DESCENT everywhere share aspects of the concept of God with those of their motherland. The people of African descent who are in diaspora, regardless of how many decades or even centuries they have lived away from the continent, will always be deemed African by race, though they belong to various nationalities. This concept is conveyed in the people's spirituality which was not destroyed though it was severely distorted due to the suffering and frustration endured during the North Atlantic slave trade and thereafter. A discussion on the Africans in "diaspora" will be limited to North America, although people of African descent are present on every continent on the face of the earth.[1] Because there is cultural continuity between the African American people and the Africans on the continent, there indeed, is an appreciable degree of similarity even though the former are now operating in the First World context while the rest of the African people are in the Third World context. It is remarkable that in spite of serious cultural disorientation, all people of African descent share basic fundamentals of the common concept of God. Several books on Africanisms among the African Americans demonstrate this point, but we will only focus on Black theology of liberation, consistent with our theme on the African origin of monotheism.

---

1. See Runoko Rashidi's "The Global African Presence." www.raceandhistory.com/historians.

THE AFRICAN CONCEPT OF GOD IN BLACK THEOLOGY: REMNANT

We concur with Dr. Asante's view that "all cultural systems are responsive to the environment; ours is no different but it is better for us because it is derived from our own historical experiences while maintaining fidelity in its best form to the African cultural system."[2] That Africans in diaspora continued to remember their traditional concepts of God from the continent makes a twofold statement: (*a*) that the African belief in God, the creator, has deep roots in the people's culture, and (*b*) that no human can obscure what God has revealed to God's own people. As a result, sharing a common concept of God serves both as a uniting element for people of African descent everywhere and a point of identity. Africans in South and North America and the islands share salient concepts of God with those on the continent since they knew God prior to being displaced and culturally disoriented. Put differently, when the bodies were enslaved, the souls were not. At least for several centuries a remnant of African culture and identity has survived.

Furthermore, theirs is a living God who makes own presence known. Even after being introduced to a Christian God, they still retained certain aspects of traditional knowledge of God especially when they quickly discerned that the Christians did not care about their condition while the universal God was concerned about their well-being. James Cone's *God of the Oppressed* makes this distinction clear. No wonder the people of African descent hold unwavering concepts of God in spite of sociopolitically harsh conditions they live through. They believe that the universal God is impartial. This, of course, is not to say that God is neutral. Rather, it means that God is fair; that God created the Black people in God's own image like everybody else; and that God and humanity are one—a message communicated through the Incarnation. This is a carry over from the African concept of God as the Great Ancestor who looks after humanity's well-being. They believe that God is the source of life. Human beings everywhere are created of the same. No one race is superior to another; this is why racial injustice was one of the bones of contention. Blacks knew they were entitled to racial equality and socioeconomic justice. These and many more indicate that the African American did not seek revenge but peace and harmony in this life and the life to come. In

---

2. Asante, *Afrocentricity*, 5.

fact, these concerns were put to test during the devastating and dehumanizing period of enslavement in North America.

Although slaves were not allowed to practice their traditional religion, their concepts of God were essentially the same as the continental traditional beliefs, with only contextual variations necessitated by the deprivation and disorientation which the slaves went through. The racism and dehumanizing conditions in the United States prior to the advent of civil rights (and which, sadly, still persist there) might have contributed to the distortion of some of the concepts of God, but by the grace of God sufficient remnants survived.

James Cone, the architect of Black liberation theology in North America, advocates the liberation of all oppressed people everywhere because God is the God of human freedom everywhere. He devoted a whole chapter in his book mentioned above to a discourse on the doctrine of God from the Black people's perspective.[3] Cone describes God as "Black" because that concept best speaks for the people of African descent in their struggle for liberation and a full humanity of which they were deprived by the dominant culture in North America. Says Cone, "The blackness of God, and everything implied by it, is the heart of the Black theology doctrine of God. There is no place in Black theology for a colorless God in a racist's society where human beings suffer precisely because of their color."[4] God, who is impartial, will intervene to ensure there is justice toward all people. For Cone, Black theology's understanding of who God is differs from the Euro-Americentric theology in that the liberation of the oppressed is the starting point. To say *God* means liberation, salvation, and survival. God is involved in history and is not a spectatorlike divinity, waiting to receive gifts from the poor as well as the rich on Sunday morning at the sound of the organ ("praise God from whom all blessings flow"). The God of the oppressed and the poor is busy continually, everywhere liberating the people.

In chapter 4 of Cone's *A Black Theology of Liberation*, from the very beginning to the end, the author articulates how all theological scholars of African descent agree with Black theology's presupposition that God is a Spiritual Reality, and not just some nebulous spiritual entity. Cone immediately refers to God and his participation in the liberation of the oppressed because he believes that the living God acts in pursuit of

---

3. See ch. 4, "God in Black Theology," in Cone, *Black Theology of Liberation*.
4. Ibid., 63.

justice and impartiality in behalf of the oppressed and the dehumanized in history. In *God of the Oppressed*, Cone discusses at some length God's involvement in the history of the economically deprived, socially bereft, and culturally marginalized. As Cone speaks in a Christian context, his position is biblically based and politically justified. In bringing the issue or problem of suffering before God, Cone's theology is consistent with African theology, which is substantively monotheistic.

Cone closes the discussion with a poem by Joseph Cotter:

> Brothers, come
> And let us go unto our God
> And when we stand before him
> I shall say—
> Lord, I do not hate,
> I am hated.
> I scourge no one, I am scourged.
> I covet no lands,
> My lands are coveted.
> I mock no peoples,
> My people are mocked.
> And [white boy] what shall you say.[5]

Unfortunately, this author cannot answer the final question in the poem. Neither can African theology. Black theology believes in a liberating God who has the power to deliver the oppressed from their spiritual and social burdens. God is the ultimate power to whom not only Black people but all people of African descent will appeal. If Africans in America did not believe that their God is God of the entire Universe, they would not appeal to such a God for their liberation in the face of one of the world's largest and most powerful military forces (the U.S. military, one of the largest in the world, may be second only to Russia or China). Thus, the Africans in diaspora believe in a God who has a record of "setting slaves free"—the God who cares about humanity so much that liberation is non-negotiable. This is the God who set the children of Israel free from the Egyptian bondage (Exod 3:1ff.), in the face of the almighty Pharaoh.[6] Now, during the Obama presidency what God did for Israel, God has

---

5. Cone cites as his source Brown, *Negro Poetry and Drama*, 64.
6. Exod 3:1ff.

done for the African American. Ol' Pharaoh has seen the oppressed set free, at least symbolically, in the person of Barack Obama.

Cone speaks from the perspective of the African people's experience in North America and throughout the world, including South Africa, which, at the time, was suffering at the hands of an oppressive apartheid government—but God's hand delivered God's people. Although his theology and Christology have been criticized for being rather racially biased, Cone argues that theology is specific and contextual. In his preface to *The Negro's God*, Mays also puts much emphasis on social context in doing theology: "The Negro's ideas of God grow out of the social situation in which he finds himself."[7] God is one who demands justice and fairness for all human beings on the face of the earth, and not only those on contractual agreement. God is relational universally.

During the hard days of slavery, the Negro people's concept of the one God was threefold: (*a*) a compensatory theology; (*b*) revolutionary theology (the silent origin of Black liberation theology); and (*c*) anthropological theology. All three emphases developed out of the point of social crisis. No wonder Cone's liberation theology found a home in the Black community and African diaspora where it was born. Moreover, the God of the Bible, consistent with impartiality, takes sides with the oppressed for their liberation.[8] Thus, Cone posits that theology is not neutral. For instance, to talk of a compensatory God is to indicate that God will take appropriate action at the most opportune time in history and reward the suffering and oppressed of the land.

Writing in 1830, David Walker affirms the "Black is beautiful" slogan; "for why should we be afraid, when God is, and will continue, (if we continue to be humble) to be on our side."[9] Note that, consistent with our theme in this book, people of color did not and do not "create" convenient gods. They continued to worship the God of their ancestors, one they had always known. Even though they might have thought to themselves, "How can we pray to our God in a strange land?" they kept in touch with their God, and their God did not forsake them but remained their God through the centuries, as American society changed with the Emancipation Proclamation (1865), the civil rights movement (1960s), and the election of President Barack Obama in 2009, their own son. In

7. Mays, *The Negro's God*, preface.
8. Exod 3:7ff.
9. Walker, *Walker's Appeal*, 14–15.

South Africa, the story is the same. Nelson Mandela was jailed for almost three decades, but when the kairos moment came, it was the prisoner who became the ruler of the land. There are some things that do not require a telescope to see them!

So both the Black liberation theologians and the novelists, the abolitionists and the civil rights advocates, all consciously focused on their own people's experience of God and God's promise to set at liberty the blind, the jailed and the poor and powerless, came to fruition. In their own respective ways, they spoke from a particular socio-politico-economic context. And, their God, who is not neutral, answered.

In connection with God's presence in the hearts and minds of the suffering, continental Africans share Cone's contention that "for God has stirred the soul of the black community, and now that community will stop at nothing to claim the freedom that is 350 years overdue."[10] Once Divine illumination occurs, nothing will hinder the dream from unfolding: not racism, not colonialism, not slavery, not ignorance, not poverty, not illiteracy, not even death upon the tree (whether lynching or Calvary), would stop the will of God who said: "Let my people go." Note that the word "my" renders Cone's perspective in *God of the Oppressed* appropriate, both exegetically and hermeneutically, because in Divine impartiality, God takes sides with the disadvantaged until "justice rolls down like a mighty river." The book of Genesis states that God did (does) not rest until everything was (is) "good."

In agreement with James Cone, another Black voice on the subject, Major Jones, author of *The Color of God: the Concept of God in Afro-American Thought*, correctly draws a contrast between Western psychological and theological ideas that set God apart as the Totally Other, and Black theology, which has concerned itself less with the question "Does God exist, and how?" than with the question "Does God care?" Furthermore, God-talk within the Black religious tradition has spoken of God as coextensive. In the Black religious experience the nature of God is both "to be" and "to let be."[11]

Major Jones' statement agrees with our overall thesis that the African monotheistic concept of God is peculiar to the continent and to people of African descent in diaspora. More specifically and contextually, the God of the African American is the same as that of Africa in that

---

10. Cone, *Black Theology of Liberation*, 108.
11. Jones, *Color of God*, 21.

caring for the suffering is a divine priority. There is an experiential kinship and solidarity between the people in diaspora and the people on the continent as they relate to God, whom they know as universal. Of course, this is not by sheer coincidence. It is the work of Divine revelation which draws a people together. In the biblical narrative, the former slave Joseph was drawn together with his siblings who had formerly "sold him" into slavery. Moses, who had put himself into exile, was brought back to his people—always for a salvific cause. In this case, God has drawn together the people of African descent who believe in the Great Provider, guarantor of good health, security, protection and abundant benevolence. It is to this God that the Igbo of West Africa, the cradle for the African Americans, offer this prayer:

> God the Creator,
> Sky and Earth,
> Sun of the Supreme Creator,
> Our Ancestor:
> It is life
> And what it is supported with—
> Wealth upon wealth—
> These we ask of you.[12]

This kind of a prayer could be uttered in West Africa and the world of people of African descent would say "Amen." Regarding continuity between Africans on the continent and those in diaspora, Dr. Peter Paris noted, "their common belief in a transcendent Divine power primordially related to them as the creator and preserver of all that is."[13] In African theology, there are no coincidences, luck or strategy. The Almighty for whom everything is in the eternal present, makes things happen for a purpose and just at the opportune moment in time. Most Africans are not deistic in their theological outlook mainly because God is not just immanent or just transcendent but is that as well as revolutionizing human conditions that need to be transformed.[14]

In fact, the majority of theologians of African descent in North America do not believe in a theistic or deistic God who removes own self from the people, leaving them to suffer at the hands of the enemy. Rather

---

12. Asante and Abarry, *African Intellectual Heritage*, 97.
13. Paris, *Spirituality of African Peoples*, 33.
14. See Exodus 3ff.

theirs is a shepherding God. As noted earlier, Africans on the continent and in diaspora believe in a God who hears the people's cry and suffering and comes down to set them free. After all, this is how God makes God's self known: acting to liberate the oppressed, the suffering the poor and the sick. Africans in America believe that God has power to deliver because when God was done delivering the people of Israel from the Egyptian bondage, God came to deliver them from a similar demon in North America before heading back to Africa south to deliver the South Africans from the debilitating cancer of apartheid. Therefore, the Africans in diaspora, like the rest on the continent, worship a God who not only deliberates but liberates the people from the dehumanizing living conditions of racism, oppression, marginalization, colonization, abject poverty, and ignorance. Theirs is a God who acts justly and with might, a God who is all-wise, all-knowing, all-present and omnibenevolent.

African religiosity finds expression and reciprocity in a God who acts in history because such involvement guarantees real peace and eternal living. For instance, James Cone talks of "the reality of the biblical God who is actively destroying everything that is against the manifestation of human dignity among black people"; a God who "has stirred the soul of the black community"; a God who "has decided to make our liberation his own. The God of Moses is also the God of Rosa Parks and Martin L. King Jr."[15] For this reason, King declared that "injustice anywhere is injustice everywhere." Black theology believes in "a God of revolution who breaks the chains of slavery"[16] and colonial thrones throughout the continent. The same God who causes rain to fall, wind to blow, and the sun to shine is the one who is pro-life in its wholeness, that is, both spiritual and physical.

Cone's concept of God as transcendent and immanent can also be translated as "one theological way of describing this reality." All human beings have a sense of the presence of God. Cone adds, "it is precisely this experience that makes them creatures who always rebel against domestication." Consequently, the Black community is thus a religious community, a community that views its liberation as the work of the divine.[17] Because God is viewed as one who cares wherever people are suffering, liberation and empowerment are attributed to God. God created African

---

15. Cone, *Black Theology of Liberation*, 108–9.
16. Ibid., 112.
17. Ibid.

people some of whom now live in diaspora to be free to become who they can be, wherever they may be. For African people in diaspora as well as on the continent, God is a part of their community. Their God is not a Sunday-worship-time-only Being. As such, the divine has a kinship relationship which nothing can ever disentangle, no, not even enslavement or colonization—the two most obvious factors that destabilized the continent in the past thousand years! In spite of all this, Blacks continue to believe that God is a reality present among them. As a Great Ancestor, God is always watching over God's people. What God has done in history is evidence of what God can do, and will do. Thus, in God, the Black community has a foretaste of eternal life through their perpetual interaction with each other.

To be a child of God had present implications. Even in the midst of suffering, it meant that God's future had broken into the slave's historical present, revealing that God had defeated evil in Jesus' crucifixion and resurrection. The slave could experience now a foretaste of that freedom which is to be fully revealed in the future.[18] According to Cone, the Black scholars' hermeneutical principle for the African understanding of God is quite different from the general Protestant interpretation espoused, for instance, by Karl Barth or Paul Tillich. Although Cone agrees with these white theologians as far as the biblical truth that Jesus Christ is the Son of God, there are aspects on which the two groups do not see eye to eye because of their respective cultural differences. Consequently there are critical points where there are radical differences. For instance, Cone parts ways with these white scholars the moment he articulates who God is, what God has done for the people of African descent, and why Christ came to this earth! Also, although all three theologians use the same basic source—the Bible—their theologizing is influenced by their social context. Furthermore, though both groups belong to the same theological discipline, their cultural differences influence their hermeneutics (with Cone using the hermeneutics of suspicion!).

Cone shares two hermeneutical principles that are generally operative in the construction of a liberation theology. 1) As a Christian theology, the doctrine of God for Blacks arises from what the Old and New Testaments say about the revealed God. We know God through Jesus Christ who is the revelation of God. Blacks also knew God beyond the Christian tradition. We understand that it is the same God whenever

18. Ibid., 92–93.

God chooses to reveal God's own self. The ideal that God has revealed freedom to be creative and to seek to fulfill God's purpose for creating humanity as an inseparable component of a full humanity is a goal that Black people seek to realize as did Christ. 2) In Black theology's biblical interpretation, God is known because God is actively involved in the liberation of oppressed Blacks everywhere. This point is not unrelated to the first one. Because Jesus reveals how God cares for the oppressed, the suffering and the poor, we can begin to understand who God is by living a life of faith in Jesus Christ. God in Black theology makes God self known through God's liberation act,[19] which leads to a full humanity. Thus being fully human is God's prime concern from creation to redemption through Jesus' crucifixion on Calvary. Achieving a full humanity is the intent of the creator who is also the author of life.[20]

Because God is believed to be actively involved in the struggle, life and death of all marginalized people, Cone perceives God to be "black like us." Although on the continent theologians do not ordinarily talk of a "Black" God or an "African" God, for that matter, they do not conceive of a God who is not dedicated to their welfare, which is why they sometimes refer to God as Great Ancestor. It is known that one's ancestors always care about own offspring. African religiosity does not know a God who is not their provider, healer, and benevolent creator. They cannot conceive of a God who does not identify with God's own creation. African religiosity regards God as its metaphorical Great Ancestor because their ancestors are in the spirit state, like God. Moreover, although ancestors did not create anything, they care for their offspring as much as God cares for God's people. Furthermore, the term ancestor is embedded with nuances of caring, protection, providing, supernatural power, welfare and prosperity. Regarding identity, Africans identify with God in so far as God is Spirit, similar to the ancestor morphology, a metaphor that provides the most profound theo-hermeneutical paradigm.

For the people of African descent, especially in southern Africa where ancestor veneration is common belief, God is a Great Spirit with whom their ancestor spirits team up and commune, in providing for the people's needs. The Mandi of Sierra Leone for instance, name God "Ngewo," Great Spirit or Great Ancestor because, as part of family, the major function of ancestors is to fend for and protect the family. In his book

19. Exod 3:1–22.
20. Cone, *Black Theology of Liberation*.

African Tradition and the Christian God, Fr. Charles Nyamiti also notes, "Another African factor from which the Christian could take much profit is the teaching that God is Ancestor."[21] This concept has great ramifications because ancestors are believed to commit themselves to the welfare of the living. They also insist on good morals which is consistent with what God has written on every heart. As discussed elsewhere in this book, not only is evil punished, it is actually eradicated because it represents potential destruction of the community. Evil threatens everyone's welfare.

Thus, the Black theologians' concept of God can be summarized in two words: *God is.* This statement condenses the concept of an active God; a God who is with own people; a God on whom humanity necessarily depends because God is all-powerful, omnipresent, and all-knowing in a way only God can be! God is the *Manyuko* (aseity) of all existence, including God's own ontology.

RELIGIOSITY AND THEOSIS

We have explored a significant range of similarities between the doctrine of God in Africans in diaspora and that of continental Africans, discovering that both teach that God acts in history because God is. Because God is, in God we are. Consequently, there shall be no more death. This statement is based on the African people's experience of God. Because God is the author of life, living in God is life eternal. This is possible because God is involved in seeing to the welfare of suffering humanity; God is almost inseparable from creation relationally though the two have their own separate identities. God is that spirit who wills to bond together all people in love and solidarity in their struggle to survive.

Preaching in the city of Philadelphia in 1834, Reverend Joseph M. Corr of the First African Episcopal Methodist Church said, "The one great aim of the address is to show that there is one Creator who has not made any discrimination in His work."[22] Emphasis was laid on the concern for human equality, as exemplified by God. If God saw fit to leave the throne in order to "dwell among us," why should human beings discriminate against each other? And why should any human being feel inferior to other people who were, like him/her, created in the image

---

21. Nyamiti, *African Tradition and the Christian God,* 16.
22. Mays, *The Negro's God,* 44.

of God? Rev. Corr's target was to eliminate from the Negro's mind any thought of inferiority. The Negro was made in the image of God, and God has prepared only one heaven for all God's children because in God's sight, everybody is equal to everybody else. Nor was Rev. Corr alone in this school of thought. Bishop Payne "was consistent in his belief that discrimination on the basis of color was against God."[23] Years later, W. E. B. DuBois would also preach strongly against injustice and inequality based on racial differences. Martin Luther King, Jr. and James Cone finally drove the point home by explicitly pointing out that discrimination was contrary to the gospel. Since Jesus was against oppression, Cone argued that he therefore took the side of the oppressed and he was "Black like us." The Gospels show us that Jesus did not discriminate. He mingled even with the Samaritans and shared the same cup of water. If this is the Jesus that Christianity purports to follow, then perhaps his followers need a new theological GPS. But the Black man saw Jesus as he really was, felt him and admired him. Thus, the slave would sing,

> Sometimes I hangs my head an' cries,
> But Jesus goin' to wipe my weepin' eyes.[24]

Black people's concept of God is expressed in various ways. For instance, Cone argues that the Incarnation disclosed the divine will "to be with humanity in our wretchedness." He adds that by accepting God's presence in Jesus as the true definition of what it is to be human, "blackness and divinity are dialectically bound together as one reality."[25] This convergence of Black experience and Jesus Christ is what we understand as the true meaning of the Incarnation—God with us. So Black people take pride in blackness. But Blacks also understand that Jesus "is with us" not in order to make us complacent, but transform humanity. In Jesus' words, "I have come so they may have life and have it to the full." Equipped with Black power, people of African descent will overcome someday soon, if they have not already.

In *The Color of God: The Concept of God in Afro-American Thought*, Major Jones concurs with other contemporary thinkers who take the position that God identifies with God's own people. Speaking in behalf of people of African descent, Major Jones says, "God, as an 'outstanding

---

23. Ibid., 51.
24. Cone, *God of the Oppressed*, 33.
25. Ibid., 35.

reality,' has a central place because he is equated with human existence itself."[26] Additionally, Jones argues that aspiring to the all-present God "is the same as aspiring to one's future, for the future is grounded in God's being."[27] This directly relates to the traditional belief that one's future, means being together not only with one's ancestors but with one's offspring as well as being in communion with the omnipresent God. Based on this belief therefore, to die or to live is being in eternity with God.

A salient point needs to be reiterated. Because monotheism is central in African concepts of God, people of African descent give God numerous names in different languages but all the names point to the same Reality (See the charts on African names of God in chapter two). This is undergirded by an African philosophy of naming which stipulates that a person is named because of one's character and circumstances surrounding his or her birth. Something is named because it is what it is, rather than what it ought to be, or what it might have been. In a philosophy of Afrocentricity, the purpose of a name is to "identify" the subject's essence. In the case of Divinity, God is named because of God's intrinsic nature that is revealed to us by God. No wonder when Moses asked for God's name, the response was descriptive: "I am who I am." Consequently, the most adequate definition of God is: God is God. We have already cautioned the reader that this definition of God is "meta-scientific." Note that for Moses, this was sufficient for him to trust God and go about the business at hand. Furthermore, there is a striking balance in that response. In defining God, the subject must be identical to the predicate due to God's simplicity.

A theological reason that compels us to reckon with this point is that in an African thought-form henotheism is not exactly the same as polytheism and these are quite distinct from monotheism. Africans who are the originators of monotheism believe in the One God who is the Spirit that sustains everything in the whole Universe; God who is conceived as omnipotent, omniscient, omnipresent, and omnibenevolent is the God who is the infinite provider. Thus a variety of names given to God merely points to different ways of worshipping, knowing and relating to the one and only living God, who is the Ultimate Reality. Put differently, God the creator is the Ultimate and yet there is a plurality of human ways of acknowledging, experiencing, naming, worshipping, and, of course,

26. Jones, *The Color of God*, 22.
27. Ibid.

interpreting (theologies) that God. When James Cone was inspired to write *Black Theology and Black Power* and *God of the Oppressed*, it is because he was speaking from his sociopolitical context where Blackness was the form through which saving grace would come.[28] This diversity should not be tampered with even by systematic theologians who tend to be faithful to a system, even at the expense of truths of ultimate reality, if such truths do not seem to conform to the theologian's method and, or system of thought. But a system is only a tool and every now and then the tool may not be ideal for the purpose. Then it is time to either just tweak or make major alterations, if not a total invention.

In the modern pluralistic and global society, Christianity has to be more than just ecumenical in its activities and theology. It needs to be what one may call "theo-ecumenical." The church must be at one with other religions whose God is identical with God, the Father of Jesus Christ, through whom and in whom all creation has its being. If Jesus did not come pointing us to himself but to the omnipresent, omniscient, and omnipotent God who is Spirit and the Truth, Lord of the universe, why should the church point people to itself? The God that some Old Testament prophets advocated when Israel became parochial; the God that St. Paul preached to the people of Athens, is theo-ecumenical or universal. There is a big different between a "Christian God" and God whom Christians worship. The latter is Lord of the universe; the former is one that Christians create in the practice of theological exclusivism. Monotheism, which originated with African religiosity, is not exclusive, but inclusive in acknowledging God who is Lord of the universe.

Jesus did not point his followers to a God who is "worshipped on this Mountain, or that hill or in Jerusalem.[29] Why should the Church point to itself not to God? For us all to become one flock under one shepherd,[30] we have to recognize various theological and religious perspectives of God's mission for humanity's salvation. If the God who revealed divinity to Abraham is the same who sent Moses on mission to liberate "my people," if the God who called prophets to preach justice is the one who sent grace through Jesus Christ, if the God who is creator and ruler of the universe is the same who revealed glory to African "primitive" peoples, then Christianity cannot declare a theological monopoly on God through

---

28. Cone, *God of the Oppressed*.
29. John 4:21.
30. John 10:16.

the name of Jesus who is God. How can we teach the world about God if we alienate the ungodly? God is the Lord of the universe. How can we be "the salt of the earth" unless we are in the world? God's particularity and universality has a unitive purpose accomplished through a diverse mission. One of the central theological challenges of our era is to bring a theological consummation to the general and special revelation, because in both instances it is God who reveals God-self. Monotheism, which originated with Africans, believes in the one God—the Incarnate God, Emmanuel, the Father of Jesus Christ. It is perfectly logical that African religiosity acknowledged God prior to knowledge of the Son. Thus, not only knowing but embracing the Son became axiomatic.

Furthermore, if Christ is the ultimate revelation of God, as many Christians believe—indeed, since Christ is God according to Trinitarian theology—Christianity ought to open doors for all God-oriented believers, rather than alienate them on the basis of a provincial theology or technical expression and ethnographical language of the faith. There is no theological basis for alienating a person who seeks God. Even orthodoxy is not a legitimate reason to keep an aspirant from joining the fellowship of believers. Jesus clearly instructs us in his words: "For he who is not against us is for us!"[31] Thus African monotheism is a paradigm not only for unity in divinity but also in diversity. True religion is not achieved only by teaching the ungodly in the name of the Christian religion, but being just peaceful, loving, forgiving, just, merciful, and most of all, obedience to God's law written on the human heart. After all, ironically, true religion is not religion in itself. Religion is a tool by which one may experience theosis—union with God.

Humanity is called to be godly and loving a neighbor the way God loves us.[32] But how can there be peace when the oppressed are suffering at the hands of those who call themselves "Christian"? How can there be justice when cupidity is rampant not only in society at large but even in the church? Obedience to God without religion is by far more soul-saving than religion without God.[33] Jesus constantly confronted and challenged hypocrisy during his day, because there were those who saw observing the Law as more than loving God and neighbor.

---

31. Mark 9:40.
32. Mark 12:31; Jas 2:8, Exod 20:17.
33. Jas 1:27.

One's cultural interpretation and expression of the gospel should not prevent the good news from incarnating in other communities.[34] Christianity cannot declare a monopoly on the theological interpretation of the word of God when God does reveal own self to anyone regardless religious affiliation, or racial classification. Rather, its challenge is to assume the Spirit of Christ, the mind of Christ. The church in Euro-America, Africa, and everywhere, should not assume the monopoly of not only the Word of God but orthodox knowledge of God because such an assumption is fallacious. Because God has revealed divinity beyond continental boundaries, the church should follow suit. God's truth knows no boundaries—be it civilization, academic, racial, or cultural. Furthermore, what God has cleansed, human beings cannot have any say but accept in obedience.

A statement by a Protestant theologian, Owen C. Thomas, that the rest of the world can only know God through Western culture is both erroneous and misleading. The truth is the God of the universe has not left any generation without some form of revelation, as Idowu noted. When Thomas says, "We can approach the Bible only in the light of the history of Western culture," he declares a hermeneutical monopoly on the Scriptures.[35] In light of the present global state of the faith, every expression of faith in God needs to be embraced because "the Kingdom of God is inside you" (Luke 17:21), that is, the whole church and even beyond the walls of the church.[36] If Christianity is to be God's instrument for the salvation of the world, it must take the form of a cognitive monotheism which traces humanity's relationship with God back to creation, rather than a political or obligatory monotheism. Put differently, it must be open and non-possessive about the word of God. Maybe Thomas and his colleagues should have said scholars may approach the Bible in the light of their respective cultures and hear what God is saying to God's own creation. This would not relativize the gospel by any means. Rather, it is contextualizing the word or making it incarnate.

However, the danger in approaching the Bible in the light of a dominant culture's values is that cultural superiority tends to take precedents over the gospel truth thereby imposing socio-cultural values. The advantage of approaching the Bible in the light of one's own culture is that,

---

34. John 10:16.
35. Thomas, *Introduction to Theology*, 54.
36. Luke 17:21.

upon good exegesis, the gospel will find root in the culture. So, a method that is suitable in one culture may not be so ideal in others. Cultural hegemony often poses challenges to the faith. Furthermore, the coming of high technology and materialism has tended to mislead many so-called First World nations into assuming that they can be independent of not only other human beings but even God; that they can control, invent, destroy, sustain, and preserve the material so well that they really do not need the spiritual. This is what is partly implied by the phrase "post-Christianity." Such idolatrous thinking must be displaced by the age-old belief and truth that there is One Living God and no other.[37] The God who was first known and worshipped by Africans, who are the founders of monotheism, has not changed because this God is immutable, eternal, and everlasting.

One hopes that Christian theological views and African Christian theology will not only complement but also strengthen each other in their affirmation of faith, thereby enriching the church's God-language and believers' God-consciousness.

PRAYER FOR THE HUMAN RACE

Hear ye, O Universe, the Lord our God is One—East and West, South and North. May divine unity in diversity influence human beings to build one people (family) with obedience and commitment to God, so that in the end, we are one people of the one God in our cultural diversity. One God, one human race. The One. So let it be.

---

37. Deut 6:4.

five

GOD, GOOD, AND EVIL

IN A BOOK DEALING with concepts of God, the subject of good and evil begs the question. So, this chapter focuses on evil as it is perceived in African belief systems. For most people of African descent, evil is treated as perplexing reality for which solutions have been established.

The presence of evil is vexing as well as unwelcome in a universe that was created by a God who is believed to be good, omniscient, omnipotent, omnipresent, perfect, omnibenevolent, and the very source of holiness. We will discuss the subject of evil from an academic perspective as well as its practical side. So the question is not whether or not evil is experienced in the everyday existence in Africa and the whole world. At the academic level, it concerns those who believe and advocate that since God is omnipotent and perfect, would God cause or endorse evil? What we have is a kind of contradiction that tends to cause a degree of embarrassment on the part of people who believe there is a moral and Almighty God who requires all people to choose goodness over evil. Our discussion here will not follow the philosophy of religion approach.

At the practical level, people experience evil to the point where they have come to realize that one needs supernatural intervention to survive in this world. Hence, reliance on God and any other supernatural beings such as the various deities and spirits including one's ancestors. The point is, whether at the academic or practical level, the question still irks: why is evil present in the world at all? Why is it that the good seem to be at the mercy of either the effects of evil or evil directly?

For the theists, the God who created the universe and declared that it was good cannot possibly be also the creator of evil, unless something is missing in the operative concept of God or evil or both. Evil cannot be part of such a creation; or, is it? Some have argued that evil is necessary for us to appreciate the good. They also contend that the color black is black to make white, white. How would one know white if black did not exist? Personally I do not find this argument convincing. In the next few pages we will discuss how people of African descent not only perceive but also deal with the question, is evil necessary for good to exist?

WHENCE EVIL?

Several scholars have stated this theological conundrum in various ways but all seem to come down to this formulation: if God is almighty, omnipotent, moral, and perfect, and if it is this God who created everything in the universe, such a God must have also created what we experience as evil, which most people of African descent actually perceive as reality. Since there is no other creator, the one and only creator must be responsible for not only the presence but continued existence of evil. However, to attribute the creation of evil to another creator or independent origin other than God is oxymoronic. Worse still, that would be inadvertently undermining God's attributes of omnipotence, perfection, omniscience, sovereignty and goodness. This would leave the theists with something less than their idea of a sovereign God.

Regarding the origin of evil, there is a tradition among the Vugusu people that traces evil back to a divinity who was created good but who decided to do evil. So from the good came the evil, a process which is consistent with the deterioration principle—from pure to impure, perfect to imperfect, goodness to evil. Mbiti says, "This evil divinity is assisted by evil spirits and all evil now comes from that lot. Thus a kind of duel exists, between good and evil forces in the world."[1] So, some societies regard all evil as caused by divinities that were created good and were initially good. In that case, does blame go to the creator or the creature that exercises own God-given freedom in immoral acts? Thus, evil can be dealt with by humans, as it is normally caused by at least one of their family members, or one of the disappointed spirits of the dead.

---

1. Mbiti, *African Religions and Philosophy*.

The prior question would be, what was the origin of what disappointed the spirit? Forde notes that among the Lovedu people, "The natural order accordingly can and must be manipulated by utilizing benevolent and nullifying malignant forces, in order to prevent evil from befalling him."[2] Thus, the creator God is exonerated, distanced from the cause or origin of evil, leaving God free to continue to enjoy God's completeness. One suspects that philosophy of religion as it is discussed in the West has not arrived at this academic height because of its limited metaphysical epistemology, its reluctance to explore the world of spirits in the universe. For those who argue that evil is not some spiritual optic illusion, evil is real. Moreover, it is not only evident among human communities but also in the spirit world where communities of spirits interact among themselves and with the living world where references to evil spirits are numerous. People of African descent consider the spiritual realities seriously because the spirit world is as real as the physical, if not more real. Indubitably, the spiritual is more immanent and transcendent than physical reality.

In many instances, evil is generally personified. Geoffrey Parrinder notes, "witchcraft is believed in everywhere in West Africa, though with varying degrees of intensity."[3] Witches are human beings who practice evil deeds which are believed to not only undermine but actually destroy social wellness of their community. In these instances, evil ceases to be a mystery because such witches are actually identifiable in some cases. But these witches will die soon or later, yet evil continues because some witches hand over the "craft" to grandchildren. Gunter Wagner observes, "Among the Vugusu, all evil things in life are ultimately ascribed to the 'black god,' the opposite of the creator God or—as he is also called—the White God."[4]

For Christian Africans, Satan who is believed to be the embodiment and cause of all evil, is said to exist and operate side by side with God.[5] This creates a curious theological scenario where God is eternal and Satan, the embodiment of evil, seems to have been made immortal also and appears to have God's permission to coexist with God eternally. While Christians immortalize evil by identifying it with an "immortal

---

2. Forde, *African Worlds*, 68.
3. Parrinder, *West African Religion*, 165.
4. Wagner, "The Abaluyia of Kavirondo (Kenya)," in Forde, *African Worlds*, 44.
5. Job 1:6–8; Luke 4:1–13.

being" (Satan), an African concept, which personifies and identifies evil in humans who are finite, makes evil mortal. Conceivably then, there will be an age when evil will cease to be. Thus, the merit of locating the origin of evil in creatures rather than in God is that there will be a time when only goodness and God remain, and remain forever. Such an ideal state is how creation began, according to several African myths of the origin of creation. Whence evil? It apparently originates from creatures which often misuse the gift of free will God gives them. Unfortunately God wills not to revoke whatever gift God gives away because God has foreknowledge. There are no surprises for God.

GOD AND GOODNESS OVERCOME EVIL

Is evil under God's control since the devil seems to live forever as God's adversary? In *African Worlds*, J. J. Maquet writes that Imana (God) is dominant, "essentially powerful and good."[6] The problem of evil is acute because there is belief in the existence of the omnipotent, omnipresent, and omniscient God. But the problem "has been solved by putting the responsibility for all evil and all suffering on agents other than Imana (God)."[7] Thus God is exempt from all allegations, which could distort our concept of God. This, for Africans, answers the question: where did evil come from? It is clear that it was not created by God and since there is no other creator, the origin of evil is other than God. We agree with Forde that evil comes from creatures such as human beings and other beings such as spirits. However, God "allows the causes of evil to act"[8] since one of the good things God did was to grant freedom to all the creatures, especially ones created in God's own image. So, when God allows causes or agents of evil to act, God does so in own divine freedom as do the agents that cause evil. In all this, however, evil cannot be misconstrued to have power over God. Nor should we deduce that God's power is compromised.

So to ask why the Almighty God would allow an adversary to be immortal almost as a result of disobedience is about the same as asking why angels do not die. Or why do all human beings eventually have to die? It is all part of God's power and will to do what God pleases. This is divine

---

6. Maquet, "The Kingdom of Ruanda," in Forde, *African Worlds*, 164–89.
7. Forde, *African Worlds*, 172.
8. Ibid.

prerogative operating within divine freedom and will. Some theists have attempted to solve this conundrum by saying that God has given human beings free will also. Therefore human beings can choose to do evil acts (like Satan) or good acts (like God) in terms of their morality. Thus God, goodness, and evil seem to cohabit, at least for a while, and the human beings are the beneficiaries.

However, the free will solution does not live long before it is challenged by the question of physical or natural evil like earthquakes, floods, deadly insects like mosquitoes, and germs that cause so many people, good and bad, to die. The human will is not a factor in these instances. In fact, the human will may actually be violated. Mosquitoes never ask for permission to bite a human being when they need a meal. Neither do they intend to kill anyone as a result of their supper. When some people give insects like mosquitoes the benefit of the doubt—that God has a purpose for their existence—one may still raise this question: why does God, then, not reveal to human beings the goodness of the mosquito so they can glorify the Maker more, just as they do when they see the sun setting over a body of water, or the majestic and splendorous Mt. Kilimanjaro in Kenya, or breathtaking roses in full bloom at Longwood Gardens in Kennett Square, Pennsylvania? Again, humanity is free to ask why, and God is also free to act the way God does, without having to be accountable to God's own creation, since God is the Ultimate. All morality begins and ends with God. To be honest to ourselves, moral and physical evil can be shown to remain a challenge whether or not free will is compatible with absolute goodness. Furthermore, physical evils create a number of distinct problems which cannot be realistically reduced to the problem of moral evil. However, good seems to prevail because God who is the source of goodness, is superior to all creation.

IS GOD LIMITED IN DIVINE OPERATIONS?

The fact of evil, whether physical or moral, still creates a problem for a strict theist: but there are several solutions for a believer who is happy to modify their theology so as to concede that God has a degree of limitations. That is, either there are some things that God has no control over once God willingly and knowingly sets them in motion, or God's will does not always prevail because there are other forces more powerful out there than divine omnipotence. Such a moderate theist would also have to argue that God is not powerful enough to create a universe that does not contain streaks of evil. If God could create such a world, it is not the one we are aware of.

The moderate theist may further concede that there are other forces which injected elements of evil or its potential, without God's permission (which really means God's omniscience and power over the universe is limited). This point would actually give credence to the existence of an immortal Satan who seems to co-exist with God and share God's sovereignty. Finally, a modest theist of this mindset would also have to concede that God is not as morally perfect as is believed to be, for God allows imperfections in a creation which God intended to be good. Or, could it be that what humanity perceives as imperfect judgment fails to see or understand what God has done in God's own best judgment? The question is, how many Christians or theists are willing to accept such views which would disclaim a God who is omnipotent, omnipresent, omniscient, moral and perfect? One's guess here is, not many, if any at all, except those who choose to deny God divine prerogative and perfect freedom. So the problem seems endless.

In fact, to concede to any of these "imperfections" would call for a redefinition of who God is. Orthodox theism defines God in such a way that God is in full control and there is no allowance for imperfections or inadequacies. It is for this reason that most African theists believe evil is not a product of God's creation. The only other solution could come from the possibility that the human reason may be incapable of comprehending God's mind, in which case, what the strict theist, or the moderate theist argues that God would not do is erroneous due to humanity's ignorance and intellectual finitude. Or, both parties may be asking moot questions. Another possible solution would be to disassociate evil from goodness and God completely. Created or not, let evil stand on its own. If evil is viewed as an illusion, let that illusion defend itself.

A PERSPECTIVE OF EVIL

Be that as it may, the African experience is that God is a reality. So is evil. It is common knowledge that goodness and evil are part of everyday experience but the two are not the same. "One of the two main concerns of Nuer religion, is 'deliverance from evil'. The Nuer ask God "remove all evil from our paths," notes Mbiti.[9] Although traditional people never

---

9. Mbiti, *Concepts of God in Africa*, 82.

blame God for the presence of evil, they "look towards God as their deliverer from evil."[10] In the majority of the ethnic groups God is not held directly or indirectly responsible for evil in the world. However, because God is omniscient, there is nothing that the agents of evil do without God's foreknowledge. They cannot hide away from this universal presence. Consequently, God can and does intervene every now and then and at will.

Although African religion has come to terms with the problem of evil, sorting it all out and ascertaining the origin and cause of evil is yet to be done. Thus, their concept of evil is contained within their concept of God since humanity, which is one of the agents of evil, is totally dependent on God.

Good and evil actually constitute a major part of traditional life, though the two seem to be diametrically opposed to each other. Like any other societies, not only would the community desire to eliminate evil but would also strive to perpetuate goodness. Thus, appealing to God who is the source of not only goodness and righteousness but justice, is viewed as the ultimate solution. God is the highest spiritual court of appeal, which is why God and evil seem to cohabitate. When a person is experiencing evil, one usually asks: why Lord? Or, one appeals to God to be set free from evil.

The Lovedu hold the notion that "misfortunes that befall men, whether sickness, barrenness, lightening that strikes men, huts, or cattle, failure of an individual's crops, or death of his children, are caused by the hatred and envy in men's hearts."[11] Thus, as already pointed out above, evil really originates from man's free will which God has given and will not withdraw. "The root of all evil is avarice" writes St. Augustine of North African. Additionally, he says "Therefore, a wicked will is the cause of all evil."[12] This confirms our earlier discussion that among Africans, there is a prevailing thinking and belief that God did not create evil, nor does God cause it to inflict humanity. In a theme on concepts of God, this is a decisive attribute. The biblical narrative of creation also substantiates this in Gen 1:25b. After creating everything, "God saw that it was good." The oral traditions give numerous other testimonies that exempt God from the question of origin of evil in the world. So, when evil strikes, many do

---

10. Ibid., 82.
11. Forde, *African Worlds*, 74–75.
12. Augustine, *On Free Choice of the Will*, 125–26.

not blame it on God. Some communities share the view of the Ila people that God "cannot be charged with an offense, cannot be accused, cannot be questioned.... He does good to all at all times."[13] Statements like these take for granted that God is above all. They do not even entertain possibilities which other schools of thought consider.

Based on several creation myths, in the literature on traditional religion and philosophy, there is a wide spread of beliefs that God gave humanity knowledge and freedom to choose right from wrong. So one operates out of that freedom, either responsibly or irresponsibly. God chooses not to withdraw that freedom once it has been given. Let us briefly discuss three spiritual origins of evil. Each type is clearly articulated.

1. Evil Spiritual Beings

There is another variation to the African thinking in connection with the origin or cause of evil. Some societies believe that evil does not originate either from God or fellow human beings but from spiritual beings that were created with such capabilities and power to cause evil. Again such spirits were not evil creations but creations capable of causing evil just as the Titanic was capable of sinking but was not crafted to subside. Mbiti's discussion of evil in this light explores various societies throughout South Sahara Africa, who share or do not concur on the origin and existence of evil.[14] However, there appears to be some consensus among most societies that such spirits are either the origin of evil or its agents.

2. The Spirit of a Disappointed Dead

The spirits of human beings who die with a disappointment in their life can be cause of evil as they try to revenge. For example if a parent was totally neglected by his family, upon death when one assumes a spiritual form of existence, one can revenge by punishing the whole family by way of perpetuating poverty or some form of misfortunes or misery with no apparent cause or explanation. By the way, not knowing why one is suffering creates some curiosity, leading to investigating the cause of suffering. This oral hermeneutic of suspicion is a peculiar form of epistemology. For example, if a daughter or son exchanges bitter words with

---

13. Mbiti, *Concepts of God in Africa*, 266.
14. Mbiti, *African Religions and Philosophy*, and *Concepts of God in Africa*.

own mother, or if a child physically assaults the parent, such action will be sure to result in a severe punishment meted out by the parent posthumously in their supernatural spiritual form of existence. Such evil or misfortune can always be traceable and even explained and justified by spirit mediums. In fact, such is not categorized as evil because it is classified as deserved punishment in return for evil done in the first place. Characteristically this happens years later after the actual act of disappointment. The good news is, the matter can be resolved since the cause is traceable. The mediator uses the sweetest language to appease the spirit of the departed, with an appeal for a good name of the clan of which the spirit is a part. Words like: "It is your own offspring, bless him instead." Or, "His glory is yours too." Or, "If you destroy him, you spite your own face. Whose name are you destroying?" Such rhetorical questions usually persuade the spirit to forgive or be reconciled.

Most Shona people, whether Christian or traditionalists, believe that failing to give one's parent a decent burial can be severely penalized by some form of inflicted evil. In instances where evil is traceable to moral irresponsibility on the part of one family member, such punishment is warranted. Minimum reparation may be demanded by the spirit through the medium's supplication. Now the issue here is not whether or not it is fair. Our task here is to establish the origin of evil, especially to demonstrate that whatever the origin is, it is not God. Furthermore, since not honoring one's parents, say by giving them indecent burial, is also a breach of the Fifth Commandment in the biblical tradition,[15] it is likely that God in God's own way also punishes those who do not honor their parents. It is interesting to note that both in the biblical and African traditions, this is the only commandment with a promise for what one gets if one obeys it. Suffice it to say, when an evil or wrong is done, punishment is generally expected to follow, after which order is restored. In fact, such punishment is not really what is meant by "evil" but is the consequence experienced as a result of doing evil deeds.

3. The Benevolent Spirit

The principle of cause and effect dominates the thinking and beliefs of many. Evil is problematic when one who is apparently innocent suffers

---

15. "Honor your father and your mother as the Lord has commanded you, so that you may live long and that it may go well with you in the land the Lord your God is giving you." Deut 5:6.

some infliction needlessly. Fortunately, in traditional thinking that does not happen either since the adherents believe that evil is always caused by something else. In traditional culture, punishment is not efficacious on an innocent person because the benevolent spirit who wields some supernatural knowledge and power protects the individual before anything ever happened. So, a benevolent spirit is like a referee or mediator. It has power to prevent evil where there is no fault.

Furthermore, even if one committed a wrong deed, it is believed that there is always a remedy for any wrong deed. For this reason, African cultures rarely use the term "sin." They generally talk in terms of a "wrong deed," which, by implication, means it can be rectified by human beings without involving God. This correction is not the same as "forgiveness" because, although the effect is similar, the processes are different.

Generally speaking, from a Christian point of view, however, any wrong deed is labeled sin against God and fellow human being or the community which would include the ancestors. Since both the traditional and the Christian religions are in the process of merging, there has been less emphasis on the term "wrongdoing," and more on "sinning" against God. As a result, the language of forgiveness rather than reparations has been on the rise. Interestingly, when misfortune strikes, most people now simply say, "God has done his will," which takes us back to the origin of evil. This language, it seems, is an attempt to avoid confrontation and reparations, and opt for forgiveness. However, such a statement is usually uttered in resignation. It is usually uttered in a context where people have come to end of their wits. It is also applied hoping to console the afflicted. But viewed from a theological perspective this could be an affirmation of God's sovereignty in spite of everything.

A BREACH OF MORAL CODE AS CAUSE OF EVIL

African societies recognize social order, peace and justice, as sacred values to be pursued, preserved and even perpetuated. So moral laws, codes, taboos and sanctions are instituted, albeit orally in preliterate communities, and are believed to be sacred. For example, if a person steals a cow, that act is a wrong deed against not just the owner but also the community since the cow belonged to a corporate body which gave custody to one person or a family. At the same time, since the thief belongs to a certain family, the whole family is affected by the consequences of the wrong act. So the entire family will suffer the consequences if they do not take action to rectify the wrong deed. Some of the laws are actually believed to have been instituted by the ancestors in generations past, and so they are perceived as inviolate. Furthermore, since the ancestors are believed to be the supernatural guardians of morality, it is simply a terrible risk to wrong such beings. One cannot afford to. A breach of any of these sacred laws "is considered evil, wrong or bad, for it is an injury or destruction to the accepted social order and peace. It must be punished by the corporate community of both the living and the departed, and God may also inflict punishment and bring about justice."[16] God is believed to be an invisible participant in community affairs, as are the ancestors and a whole pantheon of other spirits. But God is supreme.

A community is a sacred unity, whose hierarchical membership ranges from the yet unborn, the youngest child, the oldest living to the ancestors with all their hierarchy and other spirits, culminating in God, the creator in whose thought the yet unborn still reside and all other beings pre-existed. Beyond the ancestors, God is regarded as the ultimate guardian of morality—law and order, morality, ethics and justice all reside in God. Any breach of any of the moral codes, ultimately offends God. By the same token, any wrong-doing by an individual is ultimately an offense against the corporate community. Therefore, when there is an offense committed by a member of the family, it is the family's responsibility to take corrective measures to make it right, even if it means reparations. Unfortunately, these days there seems to be more emphasis on individual accountability than on the culprit's family or community. It seems the "community" called church is a community of individuals who do not actually commune. True, human reparations are always the most extreme, but communities and families work together for best results for all concerned when all amends are made by the community for the sake of every one's well-being and peace. In African philosophy and even more so theology, life after death must be a communal affair, not an individualistic one.

SACRIFICE TAKES AWAY EVIL

In the event that the community has wronged God (either through a member of the community who, say, committed murder or adultery, or

16. Mbiti, *Concepts of God in Africa*, 268.

theft, to mention a few), it is believed that God may cause a serious calamity such as drought until the society realizes that the drought is "not natural" but is a form of punishment from God who controls the rain. In order to appease God or pay the debt, traditionally the community would have to sacrifice a beast say a bull or a cow. Such a beast must be without blemish: no colors (must be one solid color), no deformities, no disease, no wounds, no spirit-possession and must be healthy. It has already been pointed out that "The guilt of one person involves his entire household including his animals and property. The pollution of the individual is corporately the pollution of those related to him whether they are human beings, animals or material goods."[17] Thus the selection of a sacrificial beast must be meticulous and the sacrifice must be done following the proper ritual.

This practice shades light on how the concept of original sin made easy sense to pre-Christian converts. Also, genealogical, biological, and spiritual aspects of purity are very crucial criteria for the selection of the ideal sacrificial animal. This highlights the necessity and unique suitability of the one and only Lamb of God, Jesus Christ, whose blood cleanses the sins of the whole world. For a sacrifice to be efficacious, the components must be morally and physically without blemish. However, even though genealogical purity and spiritual perfection are very rare among human societies, God did not settle for less. Also, it is no wonder only Jesus met such a stringent criterion. Such uniqueness also explains how it is that Jesus' blood serves as the expiation of the sins of the whole world.

In addition to all these prerequisites, the owner of the sacrifice must be known to be an honest and clean person whose social reputation in the community is undisputed. In part, the success of the sacrifice depends on the owner's integrity. The efficacy of the sacrifice depends on purity in the face of evil. Hence, goodness will always conquer evil. Consequently, only the Son of God, begotten of the Father, could meet such a criterion for a sacrifice—not the son of the carpenter Joseph of Nazareth, or of any other human being, for that matter. It took a pure sacrifice to produce such a precious gift—the gift of eternal life. Salvation from sin could not have been won from a sinful or impure sacrifice. Note that the scrupulousness with which God prepared the Calvary sacrifice is similar though by far superior to the meticulousness with which the traditionalist prepared the

---

17. Ibid., 269.

sacrifice intended to restore order, ease strained relationships and bring peace to the community.

Regarding the importance and the efficacy of a sacrifice, Dr. Tapiwa Mucherera, author of *Pastoral Care from a Third World Perspective* (2001), makes a critical observation: "Sacrifices and ritual are thus means by which order is restored."[18] Purity is necessary in order to ritually blot out evil and restore righteousness which is not cheap to secure. In the absence of goodness, evil prevails. Because Africans value order and peace, the whole community gets involved in a thorough preparation of every ritual when called for.

Again, we cannot agree with Mucherera more when he writes, "Through the ancestors, the name of God is invoked as part of the ceremony and peace meal"[19] because ancestors are a part of the community which seeks peace and order. Additionally, Mucherera admonishes, "Chaos and catastrophes may occur when there is violation of the customs, mores and religious ways of the community."[20] In agreement with Mucherera, another scholar says, "sacrifices and offerings are acts of restoring the ontological balance between God and man, the spirits and man, and the departed and the living." It is instructive to note the community will "experience misfortunes and sufferings, or fear that these will come upon them."[21]

It may also be instructive to note that while some societies perform sacrifices and offerings to "take care of business," others, though equally concerned with peace and order in their own respective community, do not, for there is no "business" for which to take care. For instance, "the Akamba," according to one very knowledgeable Amba, believe that God "does them no evil, and they see no reason, therefore, for sacrificing to him," whereas other ethnic groups believe that they are under obligation to offer sacrifices and sacred rites for every event.[22] Somewhere in the middle of the cultural pendulum are the Alur people who make occasional sacrifices to God "of the first fruits of maize and finger millet; and sacrifices of black goats when they need rains."[23] Slightly different,

---

18. Mucherera, *Pastoral Care*, 99.
19. Ibid., 99.
20. Ibid., 100.
21. Mbiti, *Concepts of God in Africa*, 179.
22. Ibid., 180.
23. Ibid., 180.

but in the same category, are the Banyarwanda who, like the Akamba, believe God is so good there is no need to offer sacrifices. However, unlike the Akamba, they believe God has two main spirits who collaborate with God, or serve as God's messengers. The Banyarwanda believe God sends these two to receive any sacrifices given. Consequently, they offer sacrifices sporadically. All these efforts to offer sacrifices stem from the general belief that being in communion with God is ultimately beneficial to humanity. But evil would be the only impediment.

Thus, almost every ethnic group has its own way of communication with God, their sole creator, Provider and Sustainer. If God had not been a real provider, the African would have wandered away in search of the true God. Thus, the God acknowledged in Africa, south of the Sahara, is creator of the universe. Evil has no role in creation, nor will it ever have one in humanity's eternally blessed communion with God.

The Spirit Hierarchy

- God
  - Deities
    - Created Spirits
      - Benevolent Spirits
      - Spirits with potential to do evil
      - Ancestor Spirits
      - Spirits of disappointed dead
        - The Living
          - The Yet Unborn
            - The Creator God

six

THEOLOGIZING A GOD CONCEPT

GOD, IN ALL VARIOUS African names, is perceived as an all-pervading omnipotent, omniscient, and omnipresent incorporeal reality. One's religio-cultural perspective and socioeconomic context largely contribute to one's concept of God, although our concept does not tell us all there is to know about God. Knowledge of God is not as contextual as concepts, which tend to be culture bound. For most people of African descent, God is known via everyday experience. Their concepts are consequently created based on what they perceive to be God's nature. In their theological reflection, God is what they experience as an all-pervading, powerful and eternal reality that no human language can fully describe, although many scholars have attempted to do so. The various names of God given by the ancient traditionalists merely point to aspects of who and what God is. We do not suppose that such names are intended to define all that God is. Rather, they only attempt to describe God's character, power and personality.

A critical reflection on African perceptions of whom and what God is, provides necessary background information in our endeavor to theologize both the traditional and modern religious concepts of God which are shared by the adherents constantly in various contexts and circumstances. Thus, what God is doing in history constitutes a major component of what ought to be the proper subject of theology. Hence, this study was not intended to be a speculation but an articulation of what God is doing as perceived by people of African descent through and in spite of what is generally regarded as so-called orthodox theology. It is important to know what those who originated monotheism perceive God as.

In addition, this is not intended to be a conclusive statement on God, for that would be a misrepresentation of the intrinsic nature of the living God. God is perceived as dynamic energy, eternally active and creative. Based on God's intrinsic nature as experienced by African communities, how any God-related data is interpreted depends on the community's experiential knowledge of Divinity. Thus, the people's religious response affords scholars fertile ground for theologizing. Again, this ensures that the God concepts discussed here are reflections of the people's experience of God, rather than merely what is dictated by logic or scientific principles. Any discussion of God concepts which is limited to logic can only produce a less-than-transcendent understanding of Divinity. African theology does not attempt to guide what God does, nor does it create a God. It does not pretend to have means by which to unveil a God either. *Revelation*, not reason alone, is the primary source of African theological epistemology. Consequently, theological concepts discussed here serve to explain in plain language, religious phenomena manifested in symbols, proverbs, songs, idioms, myths, and prayers. It is against this backdrop that we attempt to articulate and theologize the African concepts of a monotheistic God. In terms of language, I reiterate, I have made an effort to avoid gender in reference to God primarily because God is neither male nor female in the African concepts of God. God is what God is.

After several decades of studying various definitions of God, I have settled for a definition that applies only to God since God is Wholly Other. Thus, the most comprehensive and at the same time fairly accurate description of God is one where the subject and predicate balance. For instance, in defining water, one may say: Water is H_2O. In this instance, H_2O describes what water is. In the world of numbers, $2 + 3 = 5$. We agree that $2 + 3$ make 5. Both sides balance; $2 + 3$ equals 5. We could even say that $1 + 2 + 2$ equals 5 or $1 + 2 + 2$ equals $4 + 1$. The point is that once we say "equal," both sides must balance. Now with reference to a definition of God, when one says God *is*, the predicate that follows must be of equal weight to the preceding corresponding subject. The Shona of Zimbabwe say, "God is Zimuyendayenda." But they also say God is *Dziwaguru*, or God is *Mudzimu-unoera*, or God is *Nyadenga*. None of these definitions is believed to be exhaustive. Each simply points to "something about God," rather than everything that could be said about God. *Dziwaguru* is not equal to *Nyadenga*; Zimuyendayenda is not exactly the same as

Mudzimu-unoera. So, to attempt to define God, one may have to simply use the subject twice in order to capture the weight of both sides equally. Furthermore, one may not want to be bound by the rules/principles of science in every discipline. Having risen above all these language limitations, one may define God thus: "God is God."

Of course, we acknowledge that one does not define something in this manner because, whereas it is possible to equate water with H_2O, since all the components of water can be identified and analyzed with 100 percent accuracy in our laboratories, such is not possible given God's incorporeal nature. But even if we misrepresent a particular substance at one point, eventually someone will get it straight. For example, there was a time when it was accepted that the earth was flat. Then someone discovered and disseminated the truth. Regarding God, such speculation is needless because God has revealed God's own reality and identity; "I am who I am" is how God formulated it. Part of that revelation was to let humanity know that what divine manifestation humanity has received is not all there is about who and what God is, but it serves the purpose adequately. "I am who I am" indicates some unknown aspect of the entity in question. God left room for the Unknowable, most likely a dimension that the human mind cannot comprehend.

An Afrocentric epistemology entails the principle that knowing what one does not know is as valuable knowledge as knowing something in detail. For example, when I was growing up, it did not bother me a bit, to know that I did not know my father's first name. Nor did such "lack of knowledge" make me feel less love for my father, nor did I feel that I was loved less. In addition, I never doubted my father's love and care for me because I did not know him "in full." When I grew older and became more mature, certain circumstances necessitated that I know my father's first name. The new knowledge did not make me feel "more love" or "less love." In any case, the wisdom that St. Paul taps on when he says, "now we see . . . dimly, but then we shall see Him face to face" (1 Cor 13:12) is spiritual enlightenment, rather than merely factual knowledge. Again, I do not endorse "ignorance is bliss" principle in accepting not knowing God "in full."

Theology is one of the disciplines committed to a coherent language. There is no allowance for contradiction. With reference God talk, not only is coherence crucial but a pre-requite to any articulation. But coherence without truth defeats the purpose. In science, as long as there is coherence, logical conclusions can be arrived at. God is that spiritual reality that is not only greater than, but sustains everything that constitutes the universe and beyond. Since God is a transcendent reality, there is no format in which the subject can be defined in terms of time, space, weight, measurement, or volume. When we discuss some of the attributes of God in this book, we devote more time and space to discussion on God's intrinsic nature. St. Anselm's definition of God: "that than which nothing greater can be conceived," points to humanity's intuition of who God is. It does not and cannot exhaust the essence of "that than which nothing greater" can be conceived. In fact, St. Anselm's definition was crafted to accommodate the incommunicable aspect of God expressed in the phrase "that than which nothing greater can be conceived." God is "whatever" nothing greater can be conceived. Such an open-ended statement says more about God than what any name for God. For instance, Elohim, which means God Almighty, does not say it all; Jehovah-Rophe which means the Lord heals, does not say it all either. One can go on and on. An African concept of God perceives a God who transcends all boundaries—physical, metaphysical, and spatial; God whose essential nature is unknown and beyond human understanding. However, God is thought to have a personality and a will so people can "talk" or interact with God.

In African religiosity, God is attributed with certain personality traits as well as a will, without being perceived as human. This indicates that God can have a personal relationship with humanity without reducing Divinity to the level of humanity. Once more, this signifies that God is Wholly Other, yet immanent and transcendent. That human beings can talk to God opens the possibility that not only can God talk but also listen to human beings, resulting in a relationship between the creator and creation, the I-Thou type of relationship. This relational quality gives God several moral attributes.

Moral attributes

Goodness is a central moral attribute of God among most afrocentric people who believe that God is the ultimate measure of this virtue. When struck by calamity beyond their comprehension, the Shona, for example, will say: Only God knows the good reason for this happening. To say "God knows" actually is a shorthand for God knows a good reason for this to happen, or the good that will come out of all this.

God is the ultimate measure of justice, goodness, truth, and holiness, among other attributes. So, if a deed meets with God's approval, then that act is good enough. There is no higher "court of appeal" beyond God—hence the designation of Supreme Being. Among the Ila, "God is always in the right. They say that 'He cannot be charged with an offense, cannot be accused, cannot be questioned . . .'"[1] By implication, to be in the right with God also means one is in the right with one's neighbors. When everybody is right with God, then communities enjoy God's reign, peace and blessings. God, who created everything, reigns supreme in everything. If therefore God is the final judge as well as measure of goodness, no one can judge God's actions except God own self. Consequently, human beings learn to discern goodness from their sense or estimation of what God approves. According to the Bachwa, God "has laid down a code of morals and a rule of life which all good Bachwa implicitly obey."[2] Such an approach is slightly different from doing good only in order to please God. One chooses to do good for goodness's sake and derives joy out of knowing that what one has done is good because it has met all the criteria as per the Divine Command. God created human beings with a sense of good and evil. According to the Fajulu, "every person has two spirits: one is good, the other is evil. When the good spirit is properly fed, it prevents the evil spirit from doing harm."[3] God endowed humanity with the ability to distinguish between the two. Choosing good is choosing God, and choosing God is choosing goodness. Many African myths, which are forms of oral sacred texts, serve the purpose of explaining how evil came into the world. Most of the myths conclude that somewhere, one human being made a wrong judgment may be out of greed, jealousy or ignorance. According to the Ila, human behavior does not affect God's dispensing of divine goodness toward humanity, "whether they curse, whether they mock him [sic], whether they grumble at him, he does good to all at all times."[4] In God's goodness, God only grieves at their foolishness. The Ila believe that God, being a good God who cares, "takes steps to repair the damage they have done to themselves."[5]

---

1. Mbiti, *Concepts of God in Africa*, 249.
2. Ibid., 248.
3. Ibid.
4. Ibid., 249.
5. Ibid.

God's goodness is almost inseparable from divine mercy, patience, and generosity. God is merciful to the distressed because God is good. Because God is good humanity can count on God being patient with us in spite of humanity's imperfections. God is patient because God is merciful and God is merciful because God is good. When people are miserable due to whatever cause, they appeal to God's mercy. Mercy is understood to be what goodness one gets, not because one deserves the good, but because God is good. Mercy is called for to a person who stands in need but is not in a position to meet one's own need unless one gets help from elsewhere.

Because of the moral code which God has bestowed in each person, normally every human being is capable of being merciful, but due to human weaknesses, people often fall short. Only God's mercy can never be surpassed. The elderly among the Akamba always exclaim, "Oh, the God of mercy!" "Oh, if God were not the God of mercy!" If someone was so ill they could have died, one may say "If God were not the God of mercy, I would not be talking with you now." Expressions such as these simply convey how God is believed to be the "God of mercy." The Burundi say, "God is merciful" when they see God's intervention in numerous circumstances.[6] Mercy and kindness are attributed to God, who gives good health, who provides food and causes rain to fall, and who bestows a host of other good things and necessities of life. Thus God is thought of as not only generous but also compassionate and kind, because of these many acts of kindness toward human beings and the rest of creation. It is no wonder that most people of African descent do not have to be pressured to worship and praise God. There is this natural dependence upon the creator. For African people who believe that it is human to be grateful, no one has to push anyone else to give praise and glory and honor to God. Being grateful is regarded as a desirable trait in every human being.

Holiness is another unique characteristic of God. Holiness means God is totally separate from the rest of creation even though God is also perceived as transcendent and immanent. God, who has always been in existence, does not self-destruct because of God's own purity; God's nature is wholly good, righteous, perfect and self-existent because God is above any fault, sin, failure, wrong-doing and unrighteousness. God is without blemishes. Like a sacrificial animal that must be without blemish, God is pure and holy. There is no place for evil in God's nature. If God

---

6. Ibid., 31.

is the "supreme being," then God's nature and personality must be above all. It necessarily must be superior to all in maturity, wisdom, morality, being, goodness, and of course in holiness. Though rare, holiness is a trait known to the people and it tends to be most glaring with reference to God. Various examples of ritual life of Africans point to the phenomenon "that they have an awareness of God's holiness." Consequently, many people who show great respect for God's holiness try to imitate the same, thereby seeking to live a life devoid of unrighteousness, sin, wrong, and wickedness.

This idea of the universal God to whom African religion points, and believes in will not be discussed in this chapter as it requires more space than is currently available. Suffice it to say that the African concept of God does not signify private, local or even regional divinities. God is believed to be the omnipotent, omniscient and omnipresent reality soaring above all creation in superiority, quality, and sovereignty. Although African names identify God on the basis of what God has done specifically for their respective communities, such God concepts and names as demonstrated by some attributes (discussed in chapter two), present God's particularity as well as God's universality. For instance, "Nyadenga," one of the Shona people's names for God, literally means "one who owns the heavens/skies." Since the sky is everywhere, there is no place under the sun or sky where God is not known. Already this triggers another attribute—omnipresence. God is known as one who attends to a mother who is sick as well as to a clan which is plagued with some disease, or a region which is drought-stricken. God is immanent and transcendent at once.

Furthermore, this understanding of God leads to the various names of God in African languages. Such names are not mere labels as they serve to describe aspects of the character of God as well as depict people's experience of the same. As most African people believe that naming a child serves the purpose of chronicling an event surrounding the birth of the child, naming God serves to document God's authority and authenticity. The name documents the people's experience of God's activity in a particular event or a series of activities. In most cases such events are crises where God is believed to have intervened in order to save people's lives or celebrations where God's divine providence is experienced. What is apparent in any experience where the hand of God makes a difference, is God's self-revealing phenomenon characteristic of the universal God. God has revealed divine glory to all people at some point in time and in all places. However, people's responses often vary from region to region and from generation to generation. Thus, people may name God based on not only their previous experience but also fresh memories of "how they got over" crises and life-threatening predicaments—for example, the Rwandan genocide, the Atlantic slave trade in which Africans experienced not only physical but mental genocide as well.

African experience of God's acts could enrich Christian theology today because most Africans have long learned to approach the realm of God in spirit—first through their ancestral spirits, then through the Holy Spirit poured upon them by Christ who lives in spirit and truth. Throughout the continent, but especially south of the Sahara, people have acquired their awareness of God over the years primarily experientially as well as cognitively since theirs was an oral tradition. Such knowledge was public. The Ashanti proverb summarizes this well: "no one shows a child the Supreme Being." I agree with Mbiti's interpretation of this proverb: "That everybody knows of God's existence almost by instinct, and even children know Him."[7] The merit of oral tradition is that literacy is not a condition for one to receive an education. Since it costs money to receive academic education, poor people could actually be hindered from knowledge of God their creator. Yet God is the provider, protector and patriarch of all.

God is the life-giving power, which has been described by Paul Tillich as the "ground of Being." The Shona word that could match Tillich's concept, though neither term can exhaust the subject, is *Manyuko*—which I will translate, for lack of a better term, as "sourceless source" (or aseity) whose nature is to be, and serve as the cause of all that ever originated and existed. For such reality, no concept or attribute is sufficient.

Naturally, the First Cause has no time reference except to assign via negativa attributes. Thus God is conceived as *manyuko*, a source which itself does not have a source. So God is the author of not only life, but all existence. But God does not. Names that are used to address God by what God is not include: the Unknown, the Infinite, the Invincible, the Invisible, the Incomprehensible, the Immutable, the Immortal. But God is also known via anthropomorphic images. Mbiti expressed this concept when he wrote, "one of the titles by which the Akamba refer to God means Excavator, Hewer, Carver, Creator, Originator, Inventor, Architect."[8]

---

7. Ibid., 38.
8. Ibid., 45.

Regarding God's eternal attributes, most African Christians share the belief that not only is God alone the author of life, this life, but God is also author of life beyond death. Where Christianity uses eschatological language, including death and heaven, traditionalists teach transcendence, meaning spiritual continuity with God. Life simply takes on a new and different form at death and continues to exist in a more liberated context and community where disease, pain, sorrow, and even death have no effect or power.

BIBLIOGRAPHY

Abraham, W. M. E. *The Mind of Africa*. Chicago: University of Chicago Press, 1962.
Appiah-Kubi, Kofi. "Indigenous African Christian Churches: Signs of Authenticity." In *African Theology En Route*, edited by Kofi Appiah-Kubi and Sergio Torres, 117–25. Maryknoll, NY: Orbis, 1979.
———. "Jesus Christ—Some Christological Aspects from African Perspectives." In *African and Asian Contributions to Contemporary Theology*, edited by J. S. Mbiti, 51–65. Céligny, Switzerland: Ecumenical Institute, 1977.
Asante, Molefi Kete. *Afrocentricity: The Theory of Social Change*. Chicago: African American Images, 2003.
Asante, Molefi Kete, and Abu Shardow Abarry, eds. *African Intellectual Heritage: A Book of Sources*. Philadelphia: Temple University Press, 1996.
Assmann, Jan. *The Price of Monotheism*. Stanford: Stanford University Press, 2010.
Augustine. *On Free Choice of the Will*. Translated by Anna S. Benjamin and L. H. Hackstaff. Indianapolis: Bobbs-Merrill, 1964.
Baesak, Allan A. "Liberation Theology in South Africa." In *African Theology En Route*, edited by Kofi Appiah-Kubi and Sergio Torres, 169–75. Maryknoll, NY: Orbis, 1979.
Baëta, C. G., ed. *Christianity in Tropical Africa: Studies Presented and Discussed at the Seventh International African Seminar*. University of Ghana, April 1965. London: Oxford University Press, 1968.
Barrett, David. *African Initiatives in Religion*. Nairobi: East African Publishing, 1971.
———. *Schism and Renewal in Africa*. London: Oxford University Press, 1968.
Becken, Hans-Jürgen, ed. *Relevant Theology for Africa*. Durban: Lutheran Publishing House, 1973.
Bediako, Kwame. "Understanding African Theology in the Twentieth Century." *Themelios* 20 (1994) 14–20.
Behr-Sigel, Elizabeth. "Women Too Is in the Likeness of God?" Unpublished CWMC paper. Geneva: World Council of Churches, n.d.
Beyerhaus, Peter. "The Christian Approach to Ancestor Worship." *Ministry* 6 (1966) 137–45.
Biko, Steve. "Black Consciousness and the Quest for a True Humanity." *AACC Bulletin* 11 (1978) 10.

Blomjous, Joseph. "Development in Mission Thinking and Practices, 1959–1980: Inculturation and Interculturation." *African Ecclesiastical Review* 22 (1980) 393–98.

Blyden, Edward Wilmot. "Africa for the African." In *Origins of West African Nationalism*, edited by H. S. Wilson, 233–35. London: Macmillan, 1969.

Boros, L. *God Is with Us*. New York: Herder, 1967.

Breasted, James Henry. *The Dawn of Conscience*. New York: Scribner's, 1933.

Brown, David. *The Divine Trinity: Christianity and Islam*. London: Sheldon, 1969.

Brown, Sterling. *Negro Poetry and Drama*. New York: Atheneum, 1937.

Brunello, Anthony R. "Liberation Theology and Third World Social Transformation." *TransAfrica Forum* 4 (1987) 35–50.

Brunner, E. *The Mediator*. Philadelphia: Westminster, 1927.

Bujo, Benezet. *African Theology in Its Social Context*. Maryknoll, NY: Orbis, 1992.

Busia, K. A. "The African Worldview." In *Christianity and African Culture*. Conference Report of the Christian Council of the Gold Coast. Accra: CCGC, 1955.

Buthelezi, Manas. "An African Theology or a Black Theology?" In *The Challenge of Black Theology in South Africa*, edited by Basil Moore, 29–35. Atlanta: John Knox, 1974.

———. "Toward Indigenous Theology in South Africa." In *The Emergent Gospel*, edited by Sergio Torres and Virginia Fabella, 56–75. Maryknoll, NY: Orbis, 1975.

Chipenda, Jose B. "Theological Options in Africa Today." In *African Theology En Route*, edited by Kofi Appiah-Kubi and Sergio Torres, 66–72. Maryknoll, NY: Orbis, 1979.

Clark, Leon E. *Through African Eyes: Cultures in Change*. New York: Praeger, 1970.

Cone, James H. "A Black American Perspective on the Future of African Theology." In *African Theology En Route*, edited by Kofi Appiah-Kubi and Sergio Torres, 93–105. Maryknoll, NY: Orbis, 1979.

———. "Black Theology: Its Origin, Methodology, and Relationship to Third World Theologies." In *Doing Theology in a Divided World*, edited by Virginia Fabella and Sergio Torres, 93–105. Maryknoll, NY: Orbis, 1985.

———. *A Black Theology of Liberation*. Philadelphia: Lippincott, 1970.

———. *God of the Oppressed*. New York: Seabury, 1975.

Croatto, J. Severino. *Exodus: Hermeneutics of Freedom*. Maryknoll, NY: Orbis, 1981.

Cullman, Oscar. *The Christology of the New Testament*. London: SCM, 1959.

Cupitt, Don. *Taking Leave of God*. London: SCM, 1980.

Daneel, M. L. "The Christian Gospel and the Ancestor Cults." *Missionalia* 1 (1973) 46–73.

———. *The God of the Matopo Hills*. The Hague: Mouton, 1970.

———. *Quest for Belonging: Introduction to a Study of African Independent Churches*. Gweru, Zimbabwe: Mambo, 1987.

Danquah, J. B. *The Akan Doctrine of God*. London: Lutterworth, 1944.

DeCarvalho, Emilio J. M. "What Do the Africans Say That Jesus Christ Is?" *African Theological Journal* 10 (1981) 27–36.

Desai, Ram, ed. *Christianity in Africa as Seen by Africans*. Denver: A. Swallow, 1962.

Dickson, Kwesi A. "African Theology: Origin, Methodology and Content." *The Journal of Religious Thought* 32 (1975) 34–45.

———. *Theology in Africa*. Maryknoll, NY: Orbis, 1984.

Diop, Cheik Anta. *The African Origin of Civilization: Myth or Reality*. New York: L. Hill, 1974.

Dwane, S. "Christology in the Third World." *Journal of Theology for Southern Africa* 21 (1979) 3–12.
Ekeya, Bette J. M. "A Christology from the Underside." *Voices from the Third World* 17 (1988) 17–29.
Ela, Jean-Marc. *African Cry*. Maryknoll, NY: Orbis, 1986.
———. *My Faith as an African*. Maryknoll, NY: Orbis, 1988.
Enang, K. "Community and Salvation in the Nigerian Independent Churches." *Nene Zeitschrift fur missionwissenschaft* 60 (1976) 135–50.
Fasholé-Luke, E. W. "Footpaths and Signposts to African Christian Theologies." *Bulletin of African Theology* 3 (1981) 19–40.
———. "The Quest for African Christian Theologies." *Scottish Journal of Theology* 29 (1976) 159–76.
Ferkiss, Victor C. *Africa's Search for Identity*. New York: World Publishing, 1966.
Forde, Daryll, ed. *African Worlds: Studies in the Cosmological Ideas and Social Values of African Peoples*. 1954. Reprint, Münster: LIT, 1999.
Geach, P. T. *God and the Soul*. New York: Routledge & Kegan Paul, 1969.
———. *Providence and Evil*. Cambridge: Cambridge University Press, 1977.
Geisler, Norman L. "Primitive Monotheism." *Christian Apologetics Journal* 1 (1998) 4–5.
Gelfand, Michael. *The Genuine Shona: Survival Values of an African Culture*. Gweru, Zimbabwe: Mambo, 1973.
———. *The Spiritual Beliefs of the Shona*. Gweru, Zimbabwe: Mambo, 1970.
Glasswell, Mark E., and E. W. Fasholé-Luke, eds. *New Testament Christianity for Africa and the World: Essays in Honour of Harry Sawyerr*. London: SPCK, 1974.
Goba, Bonganjaalo. "An African Christian Theology: Toward a Tentative Methodology from a South African Perspective." *Journal of Theology for Southern Africa* 26 (1979) 3–12.
———. "Toward a 'Black' Ecclesiology: Insights from Sociology of Knowledge." *Missionalia* 9 (1981) 47–58.
Greilzer, David G. "Random Notes on Black Theology and African Theology." *Christian Century* 87 (September 16, 1970) 1091–93.
Hales, Roy L. "The Original World Monotheism." http://www.creationism.org/csshs/v07n2p18.htm.
Hamutyinei, M. A., and A. B. Plangger, eds. *Tsumo-Shumo: Shona Proverbial Lore and Wisdom*. Gweru, Zimbabwe: Mambo, 1974.
Hastings, Adrian. "On African Theology." *Scottish Journal of Theology* 37 (1984) 359–74.
Hayward, Victor E. W. *African Independent Church Movements*. London: Edinburgh House, 1963.
Hick, John, ed. *God Has Many Names*. London: Macmillan, 1980.
———. *The Myth of God Incarnate*. London: SCM, 1977.
Hood, Robert E. *Must God Remain Greek? Afro Cultures and God-Talk*. Minneapolis: Fortress, 1990.
Hooker, J. R. *Black Revolutionary: George Padmore's Path from Communism to Pan-Africanism*. New York: Praeger, 1967.
Horton, Robin. "African Traditional Thought and Western Science." *Africa* 37 (1967) 50–71.

Hountondji, P. *African Philosophy: Myth and Reality*. Bloomington: Indiana University Press, 1983.
House, H. Wayne. *Charts of World Religions*. Grand Rapids: Zondervan, 2006.
Idoniboye, D. E. "The Idea of an African Philosophy: The Concept of 'Spirit' in African Metaphysics." *Second Order* 2 (1973) 83–89.
Idowu, E. Bolaji. *African Traditional Religion: A Definition*. Maryknoll, NY: Orbis, 1975.
―――. "God." In *Biblical Revelation and African Beliefs*, edited by Kwesi Dickson and Paul Ellingworth, 17–29. London: Oxford University Press, 1965.
―――. *Oludumare: God in Yoruba Belief*. London: Longmans, 1962.
―――. *Olodumare: The Selfhood of the Church in Africa*. Mushin, Lagos State: Methodist Church Nigeria, n.d.
―――. *Oludumare: Towards an Indigenous Church*. London: Oxford University Press, 1965.
Imasogie, Osadolor. *Guidelines for Christian Theology in Africa*. Achimota, Ghana: Africa Christian Press, 1983.
Jahn, Janheinz. *Muntu: An Outline of the New African Culture*. Translated by Marjorie Grene. New York: Grove, 1961.
Jones, Major. *The Color of God: The Concept of God in Afro-American Thought*. Macon, GA: Mercer University Press, 1987.
Jungel, E. *God as the Mystery of the World*. London: T. & T. Clark, 1983.
Kabasele, Francois. "Christ as Ancestor and Elder Brother." In *Faces of Jesus in Africa*, edited by Robert J. Schreiter, 116–27. Maryknoll, NY: Orbis, 1991.
Kalilombe, Patrick A. "The Salvific Values of African Religions." *African Ecclesiastical Review* 21 (1979) 143–57.
―――. "Self-Reliance of the African Church: A Catholic Perspective." In *African Theology En Route*, edited by Kofi Appiah-Kubi and Sergio Torres, 36–58. Maryknoll, NY: Orbis, 1979.
Kato, Byang. *Theological Pitfalls in Africa*. Kisumu, Kenya: Evangel Publishing House, 1975.
Kiruren, M. C. *The Missionary and the Diviner: Contemporary Theologies of Christian and African Religions*. Maryknoll, NY: Orbis, 1987.
Lediga, S. P. "A Relevant Theology for Africa: A Critical Evaluation of Previous Attempts in Relevant Theology for Africa." In *Relevant Theology for Africa*, edited by Hans-Jürgen Becken. Durban: Lutheran Publishing House, 1973.
Lienhardt, Godfrey. *Divinity and Experience: The Religion of the Dinka*. London: Oxford University Press, 1961.
Long, Charles H. "Structural Similarities and Dissimilarities in Black and African Theologies." *The Journal of Religious Thought* 32 (1975) 9–24.
Lugira, Aloysius M. "African Christian Theology." *African Theological Journal* 8 (1979) 50–61.
Macquarrie, John. *In Search of Deity: An Essay in Dialectical Theism*. London: SCM, 1984.
Maimela, S. "Salvation in African Traditional Religions." *Missionalia* 13 (1985) 63–77.
Martey, Emmanuel. *African Theology: Inculturation and Liberation*. Maryknoll, NY: Orbis, 1996.
Martin, Marie-Louise. *The Biblical Concept of Messianism and Messianism in Southern Africa*. Morija, Lesotho: Morija Book Depot, 1964.
―――. *Kimbangu: An African Prophet and His Church*. Oxford: Blackwell, 1975.

———. *Prophetic Christianity in the Congo: The Church of Christ on Earth through the Prophet Simon Kimbangu*. Johannesburg: Christian Institute of Southern Africa, 1968.

Mays, Benjamin Elijah. *The Negro's God as Reflected in His Literature*. New York: Negro Universities Press, 1969.

Mbiti, John S. *African Religions and Philosophy*. London: Heinemann, 1969.

———. *Bible and Theology in African Christianity*. Nairobi: Oxford University Press, 1986.

———. "The Biblical Basis for Present Trends in African Theology." In *African Theology En Route*, edited by Kofi Appiah-Kubi and Sergio Torres, 83–94. Maryknoll, NY: Orbis, 1979.

———. *Concepts of God in Africa*. London: SPCK, 1970.

———. "The Encounter of Christian Faith and African Religion." *The Christian Century* 97 (August 1980) 817–20.

———. *The Prayers of African Religion*. Maryknoll, NY: Orbis, 1975.

———. "Some African Concepts and Christology." In *Christ and the Younger Churches*, edited by Georg F. Vicedom, 51–62. London: SPCK, 1972.

McVeigh, Malcolm J. *God in Africa: Conceptions of God in African Traditional Religion and Christianity*. Cape Cod, MA: C. Stark, 1974.

———. "Sources for an African Christian Theology." *Presence* 5 (1972) 1–15.

Milingo, E. *The World in Between: Christian Healing and the Struggle for Spiritual Survival*. Maryknoll, NY: Orbis, 1984.

Mofokeng, Takatso A. "A Black Christology: A New Beginning." *Journal of Black Theology in South Africa* 1 (1987) 1–17.

———. "The Cross in the Search for True Humanity: Theological Challenges Facing the South African Church." *Voices from the Third World* 12 (1989) 26–40.

———. *The Crucified among the Crossbearers: Towards a Black Christology*. Kampen: Kok, 1983.

Mosala, Itumeleng J. "African Traditional Beliefs and Christianity." *Journal of Theology for Southern Africa* 43 (1983) 15–34.

———. "The Relevance of African Independent Churches and Their Challenge to Black Theology." In *The Unquestionable Right to Be Free*, edited by I. J. Mosala and B. Tehagale, 91–100. Maryknoll, NY: Orbis, 1986.

———. "The Use of the Bible in Black Theology." In *The Unquestionable Right to Be Free*, edited by I. J. Mosala and B. Tehagale, 175–99. Maryknoll, NY: Orbis, 1986.

Mosha, Raymond. "The Trinity in the African Context." *Africa Theological Journal* 9 (1980) 40–47.

Moyo, Ambrose M. "The Quest for African Christian Theology and the Problem of the Relationship between Faith and Culture—The Hermeneutical Perspective." *African Theological Journal* 12 (1983) 95–108.

Mshana, Eliewaha E. "The Challenge of Black Theology and African Theology." *African Theological Journal* 5 (1972) 12–32.

Mucherera, Tapiwa. *Pastoral Care from a Third World Perspective: A Pastoral Theology of Care for the Urban Contemporary Shona in Zimbabwe*. New York: P. Lang, 2001.

Mugambi, J. N. K. *African Christian Theology: An Introduction*. Nairobi: Heinemann, 1989.

Muga, Erasto. *African Response to Western Christian Religion*. Kampala: East Africa Literature Bureau, 1975.

Mushete, Alphonse Ngindu. "The Figure of Jesus in African Theology." In *Christian Identity*, edited by Christian Duquoc and Casiano Floristan, 73–79. Concilium 196. Edinburgh: T. & T. Clark, 1988.

———. "The History of Theology in Africa: From Polemics to Critical Irenics." In *African Theology En Route*, edited by Kofi Appiah-Kubi and Sergio Torres, 23–35. Maryknoll, NY: Orbis, 1979.

Muzorewa, G. *The Origins and Development of African Theology*. Maryknoll, NY: Orbis, 1985.

———. "A Quest for an African Christology." *Journal of Black Theology in South Africa* 2 (1988) 21–34.

Nasimuyu-Wasike, Anne. "Christology and an African Woman's Experience." In *Jesus in African Christianity*, edited by J. N. K. Mugambi and Laurenti Magesa, 123–35. Nairobi: Initiatives Publishers, 1989.

Nolan, Albert. *God in South Africa: The Challenge of the Gospel*. Grand Rapids: Eerdmans, 1988.

Ntwasa, Sabelo, and Basil Moore. "The Concept of God in Black Theology." In *The Challenge of Black Theology in South Africa*, edited by Basil Moore, 18–28. Atlanta: John Knox, 1974.

Nyamiti, Charles. "African Christologies Today." In *Jesus in African Christianity*, edited by J. N. K. Mugambi and Laurenti Magesa, 17–39. Nairobi: Initiatives Publishers, 1989.

———. "The African Sense of God's Motherhood in the Light of Christian Faith." *African Ecclesiastical Review* 23 (1981) 269–74.

———. *African Tradition and the Christian God*. Eldoret, Kenya: Gaba, 1970.

———. "Approaches to African Theology." In *The Emergent Gospel*, edited by Sergio Torres and Virginia Fabella, 31–45. Maryknoll, NY: Orbis, 1978.

———. *Christ as Our Ancestor: Christology from an African Perspective*. Gweru, Zimbabwe: Mambo, 1984.

———. "The Doctrine of God." In *A Reader in African Christian Theology*, edited by John Parratt, 58–68. London: SPCK, 1987.

———. *The Scope of African Theology*. Kampala: Gaba, 1973.

———. *The Way to Christian Theology for Africa*. Eldoret, Kenya: Gaba, 1975.

Oduyoye, Mercy Amba. "An African Woman's Christ." *Voices from the Third World* 11 (1988) 119–24.

———. *Hearing and Knowing: Theological Reflections on Christianity in Africa*. Maryknoll, NY: Orbis, 1986.

Ogot, Bethwell A. "The Concept of Jok." *African Studies* 20 (1961) 123–30.

Onyewuenyi, Innocent C. *The African Origin of Greek Philosophy: An Exercise in Afrocentrism*. Nsukka: University of Nigeria Press, 1993.

Oostheizen, G. C. *Post-Christianity in Africa: A Theological and Anthropological Study*. London: C. Hurst, 1968.

———. *The Theology of a South African Messiah*. Leiden: Brill, 1967.

Paris, Peter J. *The Spirituality of African Peoples: The Search for a Common Moral Discourse*. Minneapolis: Fortress, 1995.

Parrinder, Geoffrey. *West African Religion: A Study of the Beliefs and Practices of Akan, Ewe, Yoruba, Ibo, and Kindred Peoples*. London: Epworth, 1961.

P'Bitek, Okot. *African Religions in Western Scholarship*. Nairobi: East African Literature Bureau, 1970.

Roberts, Deotis J. *A Black Political Theology.* Philadelphia: Westminster, 1974.
Sarpong, Peter. "Christianity Should Be Africanized, Not Africa Christianized." *African Ecclesiastical Review* 17 (1975) 322–36.
Sawyerr, Harry. *God: Ancestor or Creator?* London: Longmans, 1970.
———. "Jesus Christ: Universal Brother." In *African Christian Spirituality*, edited by Aylward Shorter, 65–67. Maryknoll, NY: Orbis, 1980.
———. "Salvation Reviewed from the African Situation." *Presence* 5 (1972) 1–5.
———. "Sin and Forgiveness in Africa." *Frontier* 7 (1964) 60–63.
———. "What Is African Theology? A Case for Theologia Africana." *African Theological Journal* 4 (1971) 7–24.
Schoffeleers, Matthew. "Black and African Theology in Southern Africa: A Controversy Re-examined." *Journal of Religion in Africa* 18 (1988) 99–123.
———. "Christ as the Medicine-Man and the Medicine-Man as Christ: A Tentative History of African Christological Thought." *Man and Life* 8/1–2 (1982) 11–28.
———. "Folk Christology in Africa: The Dialetics of the Nyanga Paradigm." *Journal of Religion in Africa* 19 (1989) 157–83.
Setiloane, Gabriel M. *African Theology: An Introduction.* Johannesburg: Skotaville, 1986.
———. "I Am an African." In *Third World Theologies*, edited by Gerald H. Anderson and Thomas F. Stransky, 130–31. Mission Trends 3. New York: Paulist, 1976.
———. *The Image of God among the Sotho-Tswana.* Rotterdam: A. A. Balkema, 1976.
———. "Theological Trends in Africa." *Missionalia* 8 (1980) 47–53.
———. "Where Are We in Africa Theology?" In *African Theology En Route*, edited by Kofi Appiah-Kubi and Sergio Torres, 59–65. Maryknoll, NY: Orbis, 1979.
Shorter, Aylward. *African Christian Theology: Adaptation or Incarnation?* Maryknoll, NY: Orbis, 1977.
———. *Jesus and the Witchdoctor: An Approach to Healing and Wholeness.* Maryknoll, NY: Orbis, 1988.
Smith, Edwin W., ed. *African Ideas of God.* London: Edinburgh House, 1950.
Some, Malidoma Patrice. *The Healing Wisdom of Africa.* New York: Tarcher/Putnam, 1999.
Soskice, Janet Martin. *Metaphor and Religious Language.* Oxford: Clarendon, 1985.
Stuckenbruck, Loren T. *Angel Veneration and Christology: A Study in Early Judaism and in the Christology of the Apocalypse of John.* WUNT 2/70. Tübingen: Mohr, 1995.
Sundkler, Begnt. *Bantu Prophets in South Africa.* 2nd ed. London: Published for the International African Institute by Oxford University Press, 1961.
Taylor, John V. *The Primal Vision.* London: SCM, 1963.
Thomas, George B. "Kimbanguism: Authentically African, Authentically Christian." In *African Religions: A Symposium*, edited by N. S. Booth Jr., 275–85. New York: NOK, 1977.
Thomas, Owen C. *Introduction to Theology.* Rev. ed. Wilton, CT: Morehouse-Barlow, 1983.
Thompson, P. E. S. "Reflections Upon the African Idea of God." *The Sierra Leone Bulletin of Religion* 7 (1965) 56–61.
Tutu, Desmond. "Black Theology/African Theology—Soul Mates or Antagonists?" In *Black Theology: A Documentary History, 1966–1979*, edited by Gayrand S. Wilmore and James H. Cone, 483–91. Maryknoll, NY: Orbis, 1979.
Ukpong, Justin S. *African Theologies Now: A Profile.* Eldoret, Kenya: Gaba, 1984.

Van der Merwe, W. J. *The Shona Idea of God*. Fort Victoria: Morgenster Mission, 1957.
Vidler, Alex. *Objections to Christian Belief*. London: Constable, 1963.
Walker, David. *Walker's Appeal in Four Articles: Together with a Preamble, to the Coloured Citizens of the World, but in Particular, and Very Expressly, to Those of the United States of America*. Boston: D. Walker, 1830.
Wallerstein, Immanuel. *Africa: The Politics of Independence: An Interpretation of Modern History*. New York: Vintage, 1961.
———. *Africa: The Politics of Unity*. New York: Vintage, 1972.
Wambutda, Daniel N. "Savanah Theology: A Biblical Reconsideration of the Concept of Salvation in the African Context." *Bulletin of African Theology* 3 (1981) 137–53.
Ward, Keith. *The Concept of God*. Oxford: Blackwell, 1974.
Wilmore, Gayraud, and James Cone, eds. *Black Theology: A Documentary History, 1966–1979*. Maryknoll, NY: Orbis, 1979.
Young, Josiah U. "African Theology: From 'Independence' toward Liberation." *Voices from the Third World* 10 (1987) 41–48.

NAME INDEX

Akhenaten of Armana, 9
Anselm, St., 19, 37, 46, 84
Asante, Molefi, 51
Assmann, Jan, 9, 12
Augustine, St., 73

Barth, Karl, 6, 58
Bediako, Kwame, 3
Breasted, James H., 14

Cone, James, 51, 52, 53, 54, 55, 57, 58, 59, 61, 63
Corr, Joseph M., 60, 61
Cotter, Joseph, 53

David, King, 4
Dickson, Kwesi, 29
DuBois, W. E. B., 61

Feuerbach, Ludwig, 6
Forde, Daryll, 69, 70
Frazer, James, 12
Freud, Sigmund, 6

Gaba, Christian R., 3
Geisler, Norman L., 11, 12, 14

Hales, Roy L., 14
House, H. Wayne, 16

Idoniboye, D.E., 29

Idowu, E. Bolaji, 3, 10, 65

John the Baptist, 4
Jones, Major, 55, 61, 62

Kato, Byang, 2
Kibicho, Samuel, 3
Kimbangu, Simon, 4
King, Martin Luther, Jr., 57, 61

Macquarrie, John, 6
Mandela, Nelson, 55
Maquet, J.J., 70
Marx, Karl, 6
Mays, Benjamin Elijah, 54
Mbiti, Dr. John, 11, 16, 21, 23, 27, 32, 40, 43, 44, 68, 72, 74, 88
Mucherera, Tapiwa, 79

Nyamiti, Charles, 60

Obama, Barack, 54

Paris, Peter, 56
Parks, Rosa, 57
Paul, St., 63, 83
Payne, Bishop, 61

Setiloane, Gabriel M., 3
Solle, Dorothea, 6
Solomon, King, 4

Some, Malidoma Patrice, 45

Thomas, Owen C., 65
Tillich, Paul, 6, 58, 88

Walker, David, 54

TOPICAL INDEX

Abeluyia, 45
African
    American, 36, 50, 51, 54, 55, 56
    American concept of God, 36
    Ancestry, 35, 42
    Culture, 45, 47, 51, 76
    Epistemology, 2, 27, 82, 83
    Metaphysics, 29
    Perspective, 6, 36, 40
    Religions, 10, 41
    Wisdom, 40
African Tradition and the Christian God, 60
African Worlds, 70
Akamba, 22, 44, 45, 79, 80, 86, 88
Akan (Ghana), 21, 40, 49
Alur, 79
Amba, 79
Ancestorology, 11, 28, 29, 30, 38
Angola, ix, 17
Animism, 12, 13
Aseity, 19, 26, 27, 34, 60, 88
Ashanti, 88
Athens, 63

Bachwa, 85
Bacongo, 22, 48
Balese, 39, 40
Banyarwanda, 21, 48, 80
Barundi, 45, 48
Bible, 2, 4, 54, 58, 65
Big Bang Theory, 24, 47
Black Theology and Black Power, 63

Botswana, ix, 16, 17
Burundi, ix, 17, 38, 86

Calvary, 55, 59, 78
Cameroon, 16
China, 14, 53
Christianity, 7, 9, 10
Christology, 21, 29, 54
The Church Dogmatics, 6
The Color of God: the Concept of God in Afro-American Thought, 61
Community, 1, 2, 5, 7, 17, 30, 33, 36, 43, 48, 54, 55, 57, 58, 60, 69, 73, 76, 77, 78, 79, 82, 89
Congo, ix, 3, 17, 18, 38
Cote D'Ivoire, ix, 17
Creation, 5, 8, 11, 15, 17, 19, 23, 34, 25, 26, 28, 31, 32, 33, 34, 39, 40, 41, 43, 46, 47, 59, 60, 63, 65, 68, 70, 71, 72, 73, 74, 80, 84, 86, 87
    Origin of, 70
Creator, 4, 5, 7, 8, 9, 10, 11, 13, 14, 16, 22, 23, 24, 25, 26, 27, 28, 29, 31, 33, 35, 37, 38, 40, 41, 43, 45, 47, 48, 51, 56, 59, 60, 62, 63, 68, 69, 70, 77, 80, 84, 86, 88

Democratic Republic of Congo, 3
Diaspora, x, 4, 5, 50, 51, 53, 54, 55, 56, 57, 58, 60

Distant Ancestors, 30
Dogon (Mali), 26, 32

Egypt, ix, 14
Egyptian, 11, 14, 53, 57
   Influence, 14
   Origins of monotheism, 9, 11, 14
Egyptologist, 9, 14
Ekoi (Nigeria), 26
Evil, 8, 22, 23, 39, 45, 46, 58, 60, 67, 68, 69, 70, 71, 72, 73, 74, 75, 76, 77, 78, 79, 80, 85, 86
Ethiopia, ix, 18
Ewe, 49

Fajulu, 85
Fetishism, 12, 13
First African Episcopal Methodist Church, 60
Forgotten Ancestors, 30

Ganda, 48, 49
Ghana, ix, 17, 18, 21, 40
God of the Oppressed, 53, 63
Goodness (of God), 8, 22, 23, 68, 84, 85, 86
Great Ancestor, 28, 29, 30, 47, 51, 58, 59
Guinea, 16

Hinduism, Theistic, 15
Holiness (of God), 8, 43, 44, 46, 67, 84, 86, 87

Igbo, 56
Ila, 43, 74, 85
Immediate Ancestors, 30
India, 14
Islam, 9, 10, 13, 15, 23

Jerusalem, 63
Jesus, 4, 30, 45, 46, 58, 59, 61, 63, 64, 78
Joseph of Nazareth, 78
Judaism, 7, 9, 13, 15, 23

Kagoro, 23
Karanga (Kalanga), 21, 41
Kennett Square, PA, 71
Kenya, ix, 16, 17, 71
Kpelle, 23

Lamb of God, 78
Lango, 22, 41
Lesotho, ix, 17
Liberation Theology, 8, 36, 52, 54, 58
Longwood Gardens, 71
Lovedu, 69, 73
Lozi, 48, 49
Lugbara, 39

Maasai, 16
Malawi, ix, 17
Mali, 26
Mandi, 59
Mexico, 14
Monotheism
   African, 10, 15, 16, 23, 25, 64
   Cognitive, 7, 9, 11, 13, 65
   Moral, 7, 22, 41
   Political, 9, 28
Moses, 9, 14, 28, 56, 57, 62, 63
Mt. Kilimanjaro, 71
Mozambique, ix, 17

Names for God:
   Akongo, 18
   Ajok, 18
   Akuj, 18
   Amma, 26
   Arebati, 18
   Arumgimis, 18
   Bore-Bore, 18
   Chidzachepo (or Chidziwachopo), 19, 27
   Chilenga, 18
   Chiuta, 18
   Chuku, 18, 38
   Creator of the Universe, 9, 13, 16, 22, 23
   Djakomba, 18
   Dzemawon, 18

Dziваguru, 21, 38, 41
Engai, 16, 38
Enkai, 18
Hinega, 18
Hounounga, 16
Igziabher, 18
Imana, 17, 23, 70
Inkosi, 18, 38, 42
Ishwanga, 18
Jok, 18
Katonda, 18
Katshonde, 18
Kibumba, 18
Kmvoum, 18
Kyala, 18
Kyumbi, 18
Lesa, 18
Leza, 17, 18, 38
Magano, 18
Manyuko, 26, 60
Maori, 26
Mawu, 18
Modimo/Molimo, 17, 18, 38, 42
Mulungu, 17, 18, 42
Mungo, 18
Mutangakugara, 19, 27
Muwanikwa, 19, 27
Mwari, 18, 27, 38
Ngewo, 59
Nyame, 16, 17, 18, 38
Nyadenga, 17, 38, 42
Nzambi, 17, 18, 38
Nzame, 26
Olodumare, 17, 18, 38, 42
Olorun, 18
Ondo, 18
Onyankopon, 18
Ori, 18
Osowo, 18
Owo, 18
Raluvhimba, 18
Rugaba, 18
Rugaga, 18
Ruhanga, 18
Ruwa, 18
Shoko, 18
Siezi, 18
Supreme Being, 11, 42, 85, 88

Tel, 18
Tilo, 18
Ultimate, 1, 62, 71
Unknowable, 1, 16, 19, 37, 42, 43, 46
Unkulunkulu, 17, 18, 38, 42
Utixo, 18
uZivelele, 16, 19, 38
Wari, 18
Weri, 18
Yere, 18
Zimuyendayenda, 15
Nigeria, ix, 18, 21, 26, 40
Nuer, 72

Obassi Osaw, 26
Obassi Nsi, 26
Omnibenevolent, 9, 43, 47, 57, 62, 67
Omnipresent, 9, 16, 21, 22, 24, 25, 41, 42, 47, 60, 62, 63, 67, 70, 72, 81, 87
Omnipotent, 9, 16, 20, 22, 24, 25, 39, 40, 42, 47, 62, 63, 67, 68, 70, 72, 81, 87
Orthodox, 21, 64, 65, 72, 81

Paganism, 14
Palestine, 14
Pastoral Care from a Third World Perspective, 79
Philadelphia, PA, 60
Polytheism, 10, 12, 13, 62
The Price of Monotheism, 9
Principles of Christian Theology, 6

Rwanda, ix, 17

Satan, 69, 70, 71, 72
Shahadah, 15
Shona (Zimbabwe), 2, 19, 26, 27, 37, 43, 44, 46, 47, 75, 82, 84, 87, 88
Sierra Leone, 59
Sikhism, 15
Slave trade, 8, 50, 88
Slavery, 6, 54, 55, 56, 57

Slaves, 4, 52, 53
Spirit(s), 23, 39, 67, 68, 69, 70, 74, 77, 79, 80, 85
   Ancestor Spirits, 59, 80
   Medium, 29, 75
   Possession, 46, 78
   Great Spirit 1, 2, 5, 6, 16, 29, 36, 37,
South Africa, ix, 17, 18, 21, 26, 38, 40, 54, 55
Sukuma, 49
Sumaria, 14
Systematic Theology, 6
Sudan, ix, 18

Tanzania, ix, 16, 17, 18
Tawhid, 15
Tenda (Guinea), 16

Toposa, 39

Uganda, ix, 18, 38

Vugusu, 23, 45, 68, 69

Wahungwe, 26
Witchcraft, 69

Yoruba (Nigeria), 21, 38, 40

Zambia, ix, 17, 18, 21, 41
Zimbabwe, ix, 17, 19, 21, 26, 27, 37, 38, 41, 46, 82
Zulu (South Africa), 17, 18, 21, 26, 40

SCRIPTURE INDEX

OLD TESTAMENT

Genesis
1:25b . . . 73

Exodus
3:1ff . . . 53

Deuteronomy
6:4 . . . 15

NEW TESTAMENT

Luke
7:14 . . . 46
7:16 . . . 46
8:48 . . . 45

John
3:17 . . . 3

1 Corinthians
13:12 . . . 83

www.ingramcontent.com/pod-product-compliance
Lightning Source LLC
Chambersburg PA
CBHW050841160426
43192CB00011B/2119